THE Changing Church

FINDING YOUR WAY TO GOD'S NEW THING

THE Changing Church

FINDING YOUR WAY TO GOD'S NEW THING

Daniel M. Cash and William H. Griffith

Foreword by Soozi Whitten Ford

JUDSON PRESS
PUBLISHERS SINCE 1824
VALLEY FORGE, PA

The Changing Church: Finding Your Way to God's New Thing

Cover design by Lisa Delgado.

Library of Congress Cataloging-in-Publication data
Cataloging-in-Publication Data available upon request.
Contact cip@judsonpress.com.

Printed in the U.S.A.
First printing, 2019.

We dedicate
this book to those congregations
with whom we have worked over the years
to provide meaningful change.

CONTENTS

Foreword

Actress and comedian Amy Poehler once stated what most seasoned adults already know, "The only thing we can depend on in life is that everything changes. The seasons, our partners, what we want and need. We hold hands with our high school friends and swear to never lose touch, and then we do. Change is the only constant."

Most of us have heard this funny comment about the weather: Don't like the weather in (name the location)? Wait five minutes and it will change! Or, this one about light bulbs: How many (name the religious group) does it take to change a light bulb? What? *CHANGE?*

We've laughed and joked about change and our all-too-human responses, whether it's a laughing matter or not. We often observe someone's (or some group's) resistance to change and wonder, why is that so difficult? Or, why are they so upset? After all, it's obvious to me why the change should happen, right? Maybe it's even my (or my group's) idea. Yet, when it's my turn, or my group's turn, to face and accept a change, we might resist, expecting others to exercise inordinate amounts of patience with us and to accept our reasoning as to why the change should not happen at all.

It would be simpler and easier if the change(s) we are faced with came one at a time, with plenty of time for consideration and acceptance, and with a recovery period of some length before the next change item either entered our sphere or was forced on us. We know, however, that change is a constant, and increasing, reality in our 21st century lives. Glynis LaBarre, former Transformation Strategist with the American Baptist Home Mission Societies, was fond of saying that in the last 50 years of the 20th century, the world experienced the equivalent of 1000 years of change and development. Not only were more changes taking place during that time period, but the rate of change was increasing exponentially. And that was almost 20 years ago!

Church leaders are aware of change as it has impacted the world around and within, but are often stereotypically perceived as being behind the curve in terms of responding to, or incorporating, paradigm shifts. Yet the guide book that churches claim to rely on is a record of change, from beginning to end. The Bible records the ways God has related to, loved, and redeemed all, from the brink of creation in Genesis 1:1 to the fulfillment of God's kingdom in the final pages of Revelation. Change figures prominently in the biblical story.

In *The Changing Church: Finding Your Way to God's New Thing*, Dan Cash and Bill Griffith write with the underlying assumption that God's nature is to zealously love all of creation. With that understanding, they seek to de-mystify change by exploring eight key paradigm shifts in the way God has loved and related to God's people within the overarching biblical narrative. Each chapter identifies one biblical paradigm shift (e.g. new wineskins; the shift from the old covenant to the new). The Scripture text is provided, then explored by "relating to the story" and looking at the passage in context. Change theory is introduced and explained, relative to the biblical text, and "reflection questions" for personal meditation are sprinkled throughout each chapter. Often the passage is further enhanced as either Bill or Dan reveal at least one related experience from their vast treasure trove of pastoral ministry stories. Each chapter concludes with a larger group of questions as well as extensive notes and references.

As with their previous book, *8 Questions Jesus Asked: Discipleship for Leaders*, this volume can provide a transformative experience for individual readers or groups who might read it together. Life or discipleship groups meeting on a regular basis in churches, homes, or in coffee shops will find that their reading and the resulting discussion will enhance their experience of God's redeeming love in their own lives, while at the same time they will become more conversant with key concepts in change theory. They may be further transformed by or led to consider together how best to address change and change process in their own local church experience.

The use of a personal journal for notes on paradigm shifts and change, responding to the provided questions, and reflecting on the scriptural commentary and application could be helpful for any reader. While I personally think the reading of this volume would be enhanced in a group experience, it could also be used as a guide for an individual retreat or as a foundation for a sermon or teaching series.

Dan Cash and Bill Griffith are seasoned and gifted pastoral leaders who have served local churches and people, in some fashion or another, for well over three-quarters of a century. They are both immersed in Scripture, its study and application, in a way that is evident in both of their lives. As a member of First Baptist Church of Columbus, I observed (often from a distance because of my own ministry position) how Dan led the congregation through the recent Revitalization Process. I know it was not always as easy as he made it appear, which he candidly discusses in the following chapters; nor did the church make as many changes as I personally would have hoped. The concepts they discuss here, along with a strong emphasis on a scriptural/spiritual foundation, and a well-conceived plan led the church through a healthy and hopeful process—and we are a stronger congregation because of it.

May these chapters increase your own experience of God's radical, zealous love for you, and may you move forth in the chaotic change of this world as an agent of God's redeeming peace and love. So be it.

Rev. Soozi Whitten Ford, Executive Minister
American Baptist Churches of Indiana & Kentucky

Acknowledgments

Although we both have been involved in leading churches through the process of change, we have attempted to acknowledge in this book's documentation the many resources that stimulated our thinking as we set out to write about change.

We also were inspired by the discussions and responses given to us as we led our church Men of Faith group through the original study of the material. We were very surprised by the group's eager participation in what sometimes became heavy discussion for a 6:00 a.m. breakfast gathering. It was the men's overwhelmingly positive response to the material that encouraged us to send a manuscript to Judson Press.

The staff at Judson Press, with whom we worked on our previous book, provided us with the direction and a timeline to accomplish our work in a timely manner. We especially appreciated and valued the insights and editorial guidance of our major editors, The Reverend Rebecca Irwin-Diehl and The Reverend Dr. Jini Kilgore Cockroft.

We also are very grateful for the excellent editing of two family members: Lois, Bill's wife, who took on the task of being first editor, and second editor Karen Kreider, Lois and Bill's daughter, who has a college degree in writing. The work that Lois and Karen did enabled us to send a much better manuscript to the publisher.

In addition, we are thankful for the support of Lori, Dan's wife, who cheered on Dan's early morning writing and offered continuous encouragement throughout the project.

Finally, we also must recognize the uniqueness of the relationship we share as authors. Dan currently pastors the First Baptist Church in Columbus, Indiana, where Bill was pastor from 1979–1991. Bill and his wife Lois returned to Columbus during their retirement, and Dan invited Bill to share in the leadership of the Men of Faith study group. The collaborative work of preparing the study material and working together has fostered a wonderful friendship between us. We are aware of many stories about retired pastors returning to a former church and encountering problems, so we know our relationship is not the norm. It is, however, an example of change.

Introduction

Everyone agrees that change needs to happen, but most people would like the change to look strangely like the way it is now.[1]

The morning of November 9, 2016, America and the world awakened to a major shift in politics and government. Donald J. Trump, against all predictions and polls, had just become President Elect of the United States. A surprised media and nation began to adjust their thinking to this shift in power and the potential new directions it would take. In many ways, we were witnesses to a paradigm shift.

A paradigm shift is a radical change in underlying beliefs or theory. The term was made popular by Thomas Kuhn in his book, *The Structure of Scientific Revolutions*.[2] Commenting on Kuhn's work, Richard Rohr says that "paradigm shifts become necessary when the plausibility structure of the previous paradigm becomes so full of holes and patchwork 'fixes' that a complete overhaul, which once looked utterly threatening, now appears a lifeline."[3]

Paradigms are patterns or models of behavior from which persons and groups live out their everyday lives. These patterns become our status quo—the way we do things, the way we think about things. For many years, the scientific world believed that the earth was the center of the universe. The Copernican scientific revolution changed this thinking by pointing out the holes and shifting to a new model which moved the sun, not the earth, to the center place in the universe around which all the planets, including the earth, orbit. This was a major shift in thinking. It was a paradigm shift.

Similarly, when Donald J. Trump won the presidency of the United States, he caused long-held political patterns of belief and behavior to shift. He ran as a political outsider—a celebrity businessman who had held no prior elected office. He ran an unconventional campaign, built around a populist message and the use of social media, wherein he served as the star attraction. He rejected the conventional wisdom of ground-game organization, balked at the notion of political handlers, and employed rhetoric and language that was shocking and offensive to many. In using him as an example of paradigm shift we are not endorsing his behavior or leadership but just pointing out the radical change his candidacy and election introduced.

This change became especially notable as his path to election was compared to that of his opponents. He defeated sixteen mostly conventional candidates for his party's nomination in a primary process that was anything but predictable. And, in the general election, he faced a savvy political veteran of the Democratic Party with over thirty years in government experience, identified at times by President Obama as "the most qualified candidate" ever to run for the nation's highest office. Yes, Hillary Clinton was herself a flawed candidate in many ways, but in comparison to Mr. Trump she represented the status quo of presidential aspirations and major party politics. True, she was the first woman to win a major party's nomination for the presidency. However, despite winning the three presidential debates (according to most experts), as well as out-fundraising and out-spending her opponent (and winning the nation's popular vote), she fell short of her goal of collecting the required Electoral College magic number of 270.

Mrs. Clinton, along with many others, watched in disbelief as the results rolled in and a plurality of America's voice was heard. Donald J. Trump had connected with the anger, the disappointment, and the feeling of being left behind that many Americans voiced as he traversed the country growling about how he could "make America great again." A shift of major proportions was underway. Change—discontinuous and not incremental—had carried the day, and it remains to be seen how the great American experiment of democracy will deal with this shift moving forward.

This is not a book about politics or even history. It's a book about change, specifically eight paradigm shifts that we identify in Scripture. However, before we describe these shifts and invite you to study each of them in detail, we want to suggest that change—including major paradigm change—has been a constant in the human experience.

We all have paradigms by which we define our experience of the world. These models or patterns of thinking and behaving can become settled and stagnant over time. They represent our status quo—the ordinary, routine ways by which we define and experience life. For example, I (Dan) grew up in a rural part of Indiana, with a strong understanding of the importance of one's nuclear family, the Christian faith community represented in one's local church, and a love and appreciation for country expressed in one's patriotic pride and celebration of civic holidays. My paradigm blended these three things in such a way that love of God, love of country, and love of family were at times overlapped and even intersecting. I suspect that many others of my generation with a Midwestern middle class white male upbringing would recognize this paradigm. It was reinforced by family gatherings and church services that followed the civic holiday calendar as much or more than the church calendar. For example: Mother's Day, Father's Day, and the Fourth of July carried more weight than the observance of Lent, Pentecost, or even Advent.

In the natural course of living, I moved away from my childhood environment and furthered my education through college and seminary. My seminary student internship was spent in a suburban congregation in the metropolitan Chicago area where, while worshipping and serving, my models of thinking began to be challenged.

I came into a church experience that was built around the Church or liturgical year (where the emphasis was on Advent, Christmas, Lent, Easter, and Pentecost) as opposed to what is sometimes called the Hallmark calendar (which focuses more on national holidays, like New Year's Day, Memorial Day, and the Fourth of July). I was challenged to think about my identity as a child of the kingdom of God first and foremost, and how patriotism and love of country fit with that. My worldview was broadened by interactions with persons well beyond my nuclear family. In short, I realized that others viewed and experienced life much differently than I had. They had other models and patterns from which to understand the world. Someone from an urban environment, or a single-parent home, or a non-white ethnicity, or non-American citizenry, or non-male gender identity had her own, or his own, patterns and models of thinking. Through my education and call to ministry, my paradigm was shifting, just as yours may have over the years.

Every age experiences paradigm shifts. Consider some of the big ones that Western society has witnessed, such as how we have traveled: from horse and buggy to automobile to airplane to space travel; or how we have told time: from sundials to wind-up clocks and watches to digital watches and mobile devices. Think about such technological advances as the digitalization of photography and music. And what about the ways that mobile smart phones (which are so much more than just phones) have introduced changes in communication. Do you text? Surf the web? Shop via your phone? Perhaps one of the most significant among the technological advances is social media, which has introduced huge shifts in how people are in relationship with one another.

Some suggest that another of the biggest changes we've seen is the transition from analog to digital and from wired to wireless. The implications of these changes have impacted how we live, shop, and participate in entertainment and faith. It is now virtually possible for anyone—regardless of age, education, or geography—to access anything (information, advice, entertainment, services) at any time—twenty-four hours a day, 365 days a year—from anywhere in the world.[4]

The church has not been immune to shifts and changes either. Consider how worship has changed over the years, perhaps even within your congregation. How has technology changed your approach to ministry? How is church governance shifting and changing? How are denominational life and other forms of networking different today than they were just ten or twenty years ago? In our denomination (American Baptist Churches USA), we each began and shared ministry under a hub-and-spoke model. The national office, located in Valley Forge, Pennsylvania, or one's regional office were seen as the hubs, dispensing information and ministry resources to the spokes (local churches and ministries) through national and regional staff. Today it is different. Denominational resources are vastly diminished, and staff are having to learn how to partner with local churches and ministries in new ways that revolve around grass-roots mission and ministry efforts. Local churches and ministries have access to all kinds of networks and resources that include but are not exclusive or even primary to their denominational connections. All of it has changed.

But is any of this new? Hasn't change, even change of the paradigm-shifting variety, been with us since the beginning? We believe it has. We think this type of change has companioned faith in its migratory journey over time. We think that God has used change often to gain our attention and reveal the "new thing" God is about in our midst.

Many of the changes we have identified above are external changes. How one tells time, travels, sings, and uses technology for worship may be noteworthy, but mostly they all are external to one's personal experience and belief system. The eight paradigm shifts of faith that we identify and invite you to explore in this book are not external. They are internal—changes that God has used to connect, to call forth, and to reach God's people over time. They represent a progression of the understanding of God's love that never gives up on humankind and continuously seeks to gain our attention and welcome us into a loving experience of redemption and community.

The Bible is filled with stories of change. We need only mention the Garden of Eden story to discover a first change in which we see Adam and Eve shift from a protected life in peaceful paradise to an independent life earning their own living outside of Eden. The stories of Noah and the Tower of Babel quickly follow, just a few chapters into Genesis.

In this study, we will explore the following eight paradigm shifts of faith that we believe are important for discovering the zealous nature of God's love for all people. We will begin with Jesus' parable of the new wineskins from the Gospel narratives as a means of cementing our understanding of God's approach to change. This umbrella teaching on change will set the tone for further exploration that will enable us to investigate and study the following paradigm shifts:

- New wineskins
- Incarnation
- The invitation to be born again
- Jesus' kingdom manifesto message
- The announcement of the change from the old to the new covenant
- The resurrection
- Pentecost
- The "Everybody Welcome!" session

Each chapter also will introduce a change element designed to help you, the reader, think through how persons react to and process change. These elements are intended to offer some teaching or insight from change theory to everyday conversation about change. The elements might be a model, a table, or a teaching about change that we will invite you to bring into dialogue with the biblical story and your own story of ministry, life, and change. Over the course of the book we will explore the following change-related elements:

- common human responses to change
- the Bell Curve of Change and change acceptance
- types of changes being faced today
- obstacles to change and how to face them
- processes for leading change
- covenant understandings of change
- avoiding quitting
- triggers of change
- the rate or pace of change.

The change element we would have you consider with this introduction concerns our common human responses to change. Perhaps they can best be summed up in the quote that appears at the top of this introduction: "Everyone agrees that change needs to happen, but most people would like the change to look strangely like the way it is now."[5] Social science and life experience confirm this statement and tell us that persons typically react to change through one or more of the following five behaviors:

a. Change makes them feel uncomfortable.

The old adage states, "No one likes change but a wet baby!" We find that acknowledgment of the discomfort brought on by change is a key strategy in helping persons identify and confront what they/we feel. Saying something like, "I know this may not be comfortable for us," or "I want to acknowledge that we all are feeling a little uneasy" helps to bring to the surface the feeling and put the leader and the group on the same page.

I (Bill) began my ministry in 1964 as the Minister of Education and Youth at a multiple-staff church in Paterson, New Jersey. The all-white congregation was located in a changing neighborhood that had become predominately African American, and church members, who had moved to the suburbs, and were commuting into the city to attend church. Each summer, we offered a two-week Vacation Bible School, which attracted 200 neighborhood children, but after the two weeks we had no further contact with the children or the neighborhood. I felt we needed to discuss how we might expand our contact with the children beyond the two weeks in the summer.

The members of the Christian Education Board asked me if I had any suggestions on what we might do. I shared with them my idea of having a tutoring program to provide one-on-one assistance for children in the elementary school. The response I received was silence, and I could sense this idea was making some members uncomfortable. I then shared that I wasn't completely comfortable with my own idea, because I had never done anything like this before. But I had grown up and attended school in an inner-city neighborhood in Akron, Ohio, and I knew the struggles children from such neighborhoods had in school because they received limited help at home. So, making an assumption that the children in our church's neighborhood had experiences similar to mine, I offered to explore the tutoring idea with the local elementary school principal and bring back my findings to the CE Board. The board members voiced consensus with this plan on the condition that I would make sure the principal knew we were just exploring the idea. I agreed.

Even though I agreed with the board's condition, I knew some of them still had reservations; also, I wasn't sure about the board members' level of interest. I even thought they might have been putting off sharing their true opinions with me, preferring to talk about the proposal informally outside of the board meeting.

On the other hand, the principal was very interested in the idea and confirmed that she had numerous children who needed such assistance. She suggested that if we were to do it, I should have a firm commitment from the number of people who would accept the opportunity and give her the number so she could proceed with selecting the children and networking with the parents. I mentioned to her that I felt Saturday would be the best time to do this each week, because the folks I hoped to enlist were not available immediately after school.

I took my information back to the board, and we discussed it at length. Although some still had reservations, all agreed that we should pursue it. After months of exploring and discussing the idea, sixty people volunteered to commit to one hour each Saturday morning. The principal followed through with selecting the children and providing the information to the families, and the following September the program began. It proved to be an enriching experience for all of the adults who made the commitment.

Looking back, I recall that all of us had reservations at first, but because we did not rush into the program, the participants had the necessary time to own the change and invest in it. This was a valuable learning experience for me that shaped my entire ministry and how I would approach introducing change into congregational ministry.

Reflection Questions

When were you last uncomfortable because of a change that you faced? How did you respond? What made you more comfortable moving forward?

b. We feel we are in it alone—that we are the only one being asked to make the change.

Change has an isolating influence on people. Even when we are part of a group asked to change, we tend to initially experience the change in isolation. We focus first on self and the sacrifices or disruptions that we are confronting. For example, when the Affordable Care Act, commonly known as Obamacare, caused major transformation in the health insurance industry, many people faced a change in their personal health insurance provider or coverage. For example, in ten years of current ministry with the same church, Dan has had to adjust to six different health care plans, because of residual changes that were anticipated or instigated from this law. With the election of the Trump administration and the promise to repeal Obamacare, it would appear changes in health insurance will be ongoing.

The Obamacare example simply proves the point about the sense of isolation that people experience as a reaction to change. Far from being an isolated victim, however, Dan faced this change with the entire ministry staff of the First Baptist Church of Columbus, Indiana, and with many, many others across the nation.

Reflection Questions

When did you last feel all alone in change, only to later realize that others were facing the same change? How did learning that you were not alone in facing change make a difference?

c. We think we do not have the resources to face or work through the change.

This is another common reaction to change in both individuals and groups. We often initially react to change by saying such things as, I/we don't have the time, money, knowledge, personnel, experience, energy, patience, or skill to make that change.

I (Bill) recall receiving a mailing from Eastern Baptist Theological Seminary (now Palmer) announcing their new Doctor of Ministry program back in the early '70s. I lived only twenty-five miles from the seminary and had a fleeting thought that the new program would be a good continuing education experience. I say "fleeting" because never in my wildest dreams did I ever feel that I would be interested in a doctoral program. I immediately dismissed the thought, because throughout my educational experiences I was only an average student. Knowing that, I concluded I was not doctoral material. In spite of my misgivings, however, I did not throw the program material away. A few days later, I began looking through it and was impressed with its emphasis on being a practical degree that provided an opportunity for a pastor to work with the congregation on a specific need.

As I read through the material, I saw that students were expected to attend classes for four weeks the first year while the second year was to be dedicated to independent work writing the thesis. Again, I concluded that so much time away would be a lot to ask of my congregation, since I only had been at the church for two years. I also did not know how I would be able to fulfill my duties as senior pastor, husband, and father of three while taking on an additional commitment. I concluded it would be impossible, but I still kept the program material.

A few weeks later, I received another mailing inviting pastors to Rutgers University to hear Dr. Elizabeth Kubler-Ross lecture on her latest book, *On Death and Dying*. I went because if there was one weakness in my ministry it was ministering to folks who were dying. I needed some guidance, so I signed-up for the lecture and also bought her book and read it. After the lecture, I had the opportunity to talk with Dr. Kubler-Ross, and she convinced me that a person could learn how to help those who were dying and grieving. On my drive home from that lecture, it dawned on me that if that was my weakness in ministry, then the laity in the church also must have a difficult time dealing with death and grief. Maybe the doctoral program could help me explore this topic with them. Given my reservations regarding time and cost, I concluded I would take the idea to the Pastoral Relations Committee. I felt that they also would share my reservations regarding time and costs, and that would be the end of it. To my surprise, they not only were excited about it, but they offered to fund it as my continuing education.

As I look back on that experience, I see that it was a major paradigm shift that shaped my entire ministry from that time forward. My thesis was titled "Death and Dying from the Perspective of the Caring Professions: A Curriculum Model for the Local Church." It was not only a good personal and congregational learning experience, but Judson Press invited me to work with them to have it published. In 1975, the book, *Confronting Death: Help from the Minister, Physician, Funeral Director, and Lawyer*, was published.

After thirty-five years of pastoral ministry, I retired and became a hospice chaplain and wrote two more books on death and grief. That one decision to obtain my Doctor of Ministry degree was a major paradigm shift that I almost failed to make because I thought I didn't have the resources.

Reflection Questions

What biblical leaders come to mind as you think about this reaction? Who made excuses to God (or Jesus) when being asked to make a life change? What resource shortage did they cite?

d. We revert to old behaviors as soon as the pressure is off.

This is the principle of homeostasis—the system's desire to maintain balance or the status quo. A good way to envision homeostasis is to think of a rubber band being pulled tight in one direction. As soon as the band is released it will snap back to its former rest-ing position. I (Dan) remember working alongside a congregation once in regional judicatory ministry that had been asked by its pastoral leader to make a significant change in its worship style. The pastor had gone to a large pastors' conference and become converted to a seeker-oriented approach to worship. Upon returning home, he implemented some of these changes on his own authority, resulting in the removal of all hymnals, installation of a projector and screen, and replacement of the church's organ with an electronic keyboard. The pastor did not get to enjoy the fruits of his labor, however, because he was terminated the first Sunday after he introduced these changes. Furthermore, before that day was over, the hymnals were back in place, the projector and screen were dismantled, and the organ was restored while the electronic keyboard was sent to storage. This anecdotal account of change may say more about a lack of process and poor implementation, but it clearly also demonstrates the restoration of homeostasis.

Reflection Questions

When have you seen a person or system revert to old behaviors when the pressure to change was in some way lessoned or turned off? Do you have a personal story of such behavior?

e. We can accept only so much change at one time.

Life today is filled with change. People face change in the workplace, in their healthcare, in the use and availability of technology, in the marketplace, and in social relationships. Is it any wonder that change is often resisted in the church? After all, for many the church feels like the last safe bastion of constancy, where all of us who dread change can take refuge. Sensitivity to both the volume and rate of change is important for those of us who lead others. As one of Dan's childhood pastoral leaders often told him, "Hasten slowly, lad (when making change). Hasten slowly."

Reflection Questions
When have you experienced a high volume and/or rate of change in your life? How has this made you feel?

Finally, each chapter comes with discussion questions designed to help you think through the content of the chapter individually or with a small group or class. We hope that you will utilize these questions to spark conversation and thought that is contextual to the challenges, paradigm shifts, and changes that you are facing. Your willingness to engage with this study may be an indicator that you know change is a constant companion to life. You also may be experiencing change that is paradigmatic in nature. What better way to learn and reflect on this change than through a discovery of faith's great paradigm shifts.

Questions for Group Discussion or Personal Reflection

1. How do you usually react to change? Please give examples.
2. What would you put on a list of the major paradigm shifts that have taken place on the world stage during your lifetime?
3. Now let's think more personally. What would be on your list of personal paradigm shifts in your lifetime? How have these paradigm shifts caused you to think and live differently?
4. Which of the above changes did you resist the most? Why?
5. Which change has had the most influence in shaping your life?
6. In the narrative of this introduction, we mentioned a couple of biblical shifts that happened within the first chapters of Genesis (Noah's story and the Tower of Babel). What other biblical stories come to mind that you would consider being major paradigm shifts of faith?
7. Which of the five typical behavioral reactions to change listed above do you most identify with? Why? What other reaction have you often witnessed in groups when change is introduced?

Notes

1. Gary V. Nelson and Peter M. Dickens *Leading in Disorienting Times: Navigating Church and Organizational Change* (Duluth, GA: Chalice Press: TCP Books, 2015), 74.

2. Thomas Kuhn, *The Structure of Scientific Revolutions* (Chicago: University of Chicago Press, 1962).

3. Richard Rohr and Mike Morrell, *The Divine Dance: The Trinity and Your Transformation* (New Kensington, PA: Whitaker House, 2016), 36.

4. For a discussion of the "The 4 'Anys'" see the The Gumblog at: http://www.bigbluegumball.com/the-gumblog/2012/6/5/the-biggest-paradigm-shift-of-our-generation-the-4-anys.html.

5. Nelson and Dickens, 74.

CHAPTER ONE

New Wineskins

Luke 5:33-39

> *[M]ost credible evidence suggests . . . that the rate of environmental movement will increase and that the pressures on organizations to transform themselves will grow over the next decades.*[1]

Scripture Encounter

33Then they said to him, "John's disciples, like the disciples of the
Pharisees, frequently fast and pray, but your disciples eat and drink."
34Jesus said to them, "You cannot make wedding guests fast while the
bridegroom is with them, can you? 35The days will come when the bride-
groom will be taken away from them, and then they will fast in those
days." 36He also told them a parable: "No one tears a piece from a new
garment and sews it on an old garment; otherwise the new will be torn,
and the piece from the new will not match the old. 37And no one puts new
wine into old wineskins; otherwise the new wine will burst the skins and
will be spilled, and the skins will be destroyed. 38But new wine must be
put into fresh wineskins. 39And no one after drinking old wine desires new
wine, but says, 'The old is good.'"

Relating to the Story

"Change" can be both a scary word and concept. As we pointed out in the introduction to this book, most people do not welcome change. You may have heard the question asked: "How many Baptists (substitute your group here) does it take to change a light bulb?" What's the answer? "Change!?"

Jesus recognized resistance to change among his listeners, including both his critics and his disciples. These individuals, like most of us, were comfortable with the status quo, yet Jesus brought a message about the Kingdom of God that was centered on the need to change. It is not that he wanted to rid the world of everything old or traditional. Just the opposite, Jesus valued tradition, but he taught the need to change so that persons did not live in the past and fail to see the saving acts of God taking place in the here and now.

In this chapter, we will focus on an encounter Jesus had with some of the religious leaders of his day. They objected to the changes in behavior, different from the norms of their day, that they noted among Jesus and his disciples. In response to their criticism, Jesus offered two metaphors on change. When taken together with the surrounding context in which they were shared, these metaphors enable us to see the major paradigm shift he introduced.

Before we explore the story, we would like you, the reader, to consider some of the changes you have had to process over your lifetime when it comes to your religious practice. *What do you do differently in the daily or weekly living out of your faith today than you did in the past? What has changed in your practice? What has changed in your thinking? What changes in faith or discipleship do you struggle with?* Perhaps it will help if we offer a couple of examples.

I (Bill) grew up in a very fundamentalist religious home where I was not allowed to go to the movies or dances or attend any sporting event on Sunday. I remember questioning my dad about this one Sunday afternoon as we were tossing a football around in the backyard. I wanted to know why it was ok to watch a game on television, or play catch in the backyard, but not to go and sit and watch others do it. I didn't like this restriction, because it kept me from going to the Soap Box Derby held on Sunday in our city of Akron, Ohio. My dad did not have an answer that satisfied me.

Alcohol and smoking also were on the "no-no" sin list. I recall one evening when I was a child that while saying my prayers with my mother I prayed for one of my uncles by name, asking God to save him. After I said amen, my mother asked me why I prayed for his salvation since he was a Christian. My only answer was, "If he smokes, he's a sinner and needs to be saved." She was not able to explain the contradiction I was feeling. These experiences illustrate religious standards that were embedded in my Christian beliefs. As I grew older, I discovered different answers, but only as an adult did I reexamine my beliefs and experience a paradigm shift.

For me, (Dan), the practice of Sabbath keeping during my upbringing included prohibition against doing any real manual work on a Sunday. I was reared in a rural, farming community where it was known that good Christian farmers did not work in the fields on Sunday, just as good Christian homeowners got the grass cut on Saturday or waited for a weeknight. As an adult, living in the fast-paced society of today, filled with busy Saturdays, I can see how persons of faith might question these practices; yet it would be difficult for me, even now, to modify my own behavior when it comes to lawn care.

Reflection Questions

What about you? What has changed in your practice? What changes do you see happening around you, in your life and faith, that you struggle with?

The Scripture in Context

As Jesus' opponents watched his behavior over time, they began to build a list of concerns in their case against him. His choice of disciples was troubling in that he surrounded himself with a group that included uneducated, common working-class men. Fishermen from Galilee were among this group (Luke 5:1-10), but perhaps more troubling than this was his inclusion of a tax collector named Levi (Luke 5:27ff).

Tax collectors were known to exploit their Jewish neighbors and countrymen as they colluded with Rome to raise revenue. This collaboration with uncircumcised Gentiles rendered a tax collector impure in the eyes of the Jewish law and its teachers. Tax collectors' status on the lowest rungs of the Jewish community originated from the life they led, which might have included anything from the practice of charging high interest rates in their collection work to making a personal profit by whatever means possible.

Like the fishermen in Jesus' group, a tax collector (such as Levi) would only have learned basic teachings of the Jewish faith and were considered far inferior to the devout religious class of scribes and Pharisees. The consensus of opinion regarding the disciples was that they were uneducated and ordinary men (Acts 4:13).

Furthermore, these men, the disciples of Jesus, were not keeping the customary practices of fasting that even John the Baptist's disciples followed. Jesus eating in the home of a tax collector and mingling with his cast of associates was something the Pharisees found disgusting and diametrically opposite of the behavior expected of a rabbi. This change in behavior was too much to swallow, and it led Jesus' opponents to launch their verbal attack: "Why do you eat and drink with tax collectors and sinners?" (Luke 5:30b). "Why don't your disciples fast and pray (like John's disciples and those of the Pharisees)?" (Luke 5:33).

Jesus' response to their questions did little to endear him to them. First, he offered the comparison of a physician, suggesting that a medical doctor would always be found with those who are sick (Luke 5:31). Let's take a moment to consider this shift in practice and thinking. Jesus had just put forward a poignant critique in both word and practice to the religious traditions of his contemporaries. Their practice of faith had been built on purity, separation, and a strict adherence to the law. They took pride in their disassociation with those whom they and the law identified as sinners.

The Pharisees remind us of the story of the poor man who went into a large city church dressed in very shabby clothing. At the conclusion of the service, the pastor said to him as he was leaving, "Next Sunday, see if you can find something better to wear to worship." The next Sunday he came back wearing the same clothes. As he was leaving, the pastor said, "I suggest you pray and ask God what you should wear when you come to this church." The following Sunday the man returned in the same clothes, and as he was leaving, the pastor said in a very stern voice, "I thought I asked you to pray and ask God what was appropriate to wear to church." And the man replied, "I did, and God said he didn't know because he's never been in this church."

Religious practice, for the religious leaders of Jesus' day, was as much about what one did not do as it was about what one did. For Jesus to both model and teach a different way of engagement and faith practice was a shift—and a major one at that—from what these men, steeped in the practices of Judaism, had come to take pride in. Furthermore, to set aside the practice of fasting and prayer in favor of feasting and joining with sinners was a terrific offense and challenge to the system and design of their day.

Relating to the Story

Lest we be too quick to pile on and cast aspersions at the religious elites of Jesus' day, let us offer a contemporary story that in some ways parallels our Scripture narrative. In our community of Columbus, Indiana, the local churches provide a hot meal each day of the week through a collaborative ecumenical effort. These meals mostly are attended by those who are homeless and/or living on limited resources with no real financial margin. The meals bring together (for the most part) two groups of people: those who partake of the meal, who represent the poor and lower economic group of the community, and the church folk, most of whom are the upper-middle-income group who provide and serve the meals. This practice of providing and consuming hot meals has been going on for years in our community.

We have noticed a disturbing practice of separation that plays out. When members of our congregation go to provide and serve a meal, we generally do so from behind a counter that separates us from our guests who have come to receive the meal. Furthermore, it is customary for those who serve to also eat the meal after we have served all the guests. But this, too, is done in an "us" and "them" fashion, with our team literally eating off by ourselves, separate from the community participants.

Through a men's small group study, we began to point out this pattern of behavior and challenge our group to change. What if, we suggested, rather than remain divided by the serving barrier and custom, we went to sit among the community guests? What if we divided up and sat one or two to a table among them? What if we learned their names? Listened to their stories? Engaged them in conversation? Could some intentional practices for behavioral changes eventually lead to a change in thinking? The jury is still out on this experiment, but we are happy to report that persons are willingly engaging in it.

Reflection Questions

Where in your own practice of ministry have you seen a similar divide or separation? What steps might Jesus' example in Luke 5 encourage you and your group to take?

The Scripture in Context

Having offered his audience the metaphor of a physician ministering to the sick, Jesus next tackled their criticism that his disciples did not fast. This time he introduced the analogy of a wedding feast. Weddings in Jesus' time were occasions for celebration, just as they are now. Great thought and detail went into the planning of both the ceremony and the accompanying celebratory feast. People knew what to expect when they went to a wedding—joy, celebration, eating, and drinking—feasting, not fasting!

When Jesus compared his kingdom ministry to that of a bridegroom among his guests at the wedding feast, he drew on common knowledge and practice. It would have been ridiculous for the bridegroom, or any other members of the wedding party, to proclaim a fast at what obviously should be a feast. There would be a time and place for fasting, but this was the time for feasting!

I (Dan) especially can relate to this analogy. My wife and I recently threw a wedding celebration for our oldest daughter. We planned a wedding over a period of several months that would accommodate three hundred guests. With our daughter's and her fiancé's full endorsement, we had designed a day that would be centered at our church where a meaningful ceremony would be followed by a celebratory reception—a feast.

The ceremony took place in the sanctuary of the church facility, and the reception was held on the back lawn under a large tent. It was a terrific day. The bride and groom were enchanting, the wedding party complimentary, the ceremony meaningful as hoped, and the reception a big blow-out party. But, my oh my, did my wife and I ever become more empathetic to the parents of young people who are getting married! Preparation for the wedding and reception consumed our days leading up to the event. Once the tent was erected, it needed to be staged, lighted, decorated, fitted with sound, and prepared to accommodate the wedding guests. All of that happened, thanks to an army of volunteers and family that made it possible for us to enjoy the event.

But as the reception was winding down and guests were beginning to go out into the cool autumn night, that same army of volunteers and family began to assist with tearing down and packing up things. I was grateful for their help but found that I could not join in so long as the bride and groom were still present. I wanted to enjoy them and their happiness, not engage in work that could wait until later. There would be, and was, time for the work in the hours and days to come; we could fast and unfasten and break down and pack up later. This was a time for dancing and feasting. "The days will come when the bridegroom [and bride] will be taken away from them, and then they will fast in those days" (Luke 5:35).

In this response to his critics, Jesus was not denying the importance of fasting and prayer. He believed in that tradition and honored it as part of his own practice of faith. What he questioned was the timing. Just as a wedding celebration is not the time for fasting, he suggested that his presence with the disciples and others was to be a joyful time—a time of feasting and celebration—a time to declare that the kingdom of God had arrived.

Jesus' Two Metaphors

To further his point, Jesus next shared two brief metaphors, which would have been familiar to his listeners.[2] Both metaphors point to the fact that the *new*, whether it be a piece of fabric or a container of wine, must not be used with the *old*, because the results would lead to disaster. The word translated as "old" here is a term that designates something whose time is past, something that has become worn out and has therefore lost its usefulness.[3]

The old Jewish system had lost its usefulness. It had served its time, and now its time had passed. New fabric would shrink when washed and, because the old was already shrunken, the force would pull the new away from the old, and both would be destroyed. The same outcome was forecast with reference to new wine and leather wineskins. The *old* wine was once new and had stretched the old wineskin when the wine fermented. To put new wine, which still was fermenting, in that old wineskin, now rigid and not pliable, would make it give way and break, causing both the wine and wineskin to be lost. Both of Jesus' metaphors (cloth and wine) call for new resources, new approaches, and a new paradigm by which to participate in the faith.

Jesus offered a critique of his critics and their practice of faith. The *old* garment (the law) had been misused by the many rules that were added, meaning it was torn. This was the state of Judaism as Jesus saw it operating during his day. Simply putting a *new* patch on this *old* garment only would make things worse. We must not overlook that nowhere in Jesus' teaching was he attempting to convince persons that Judaism was not relevant. He attended the Synagogue and Temple services and festivals. He often quoted from the Torah, the prophets, and the Psalms. He did not want that container to be destroyed.

However, the old religious teachings offered no hope to persons like Levi and his friends, who were considered to be impure, while Jesus' compassion and caring offered a *new* way—a way that was impossible to incorporate into the *old* traditions. John's disciples, as faithful as they were to the fasting law, had kept their *old* expectations, not considering that God could do a *new thing*. It wasn't the fasting that was wrong; it was the timing in not realizing that Jesus was ushering in a *new* way, which he identified as the kingdom of God. In choosing fishermen, a tax collector, and other common people, Jesus was putting his new wine message forward through new messengers (wineskins), perhaps knowing as we might say today, "You can't teach an old dog new tricks." Change had been introduced. A paradigm shift was afoot.

New forms of music (drums and guitars) that have been introduced in many worship services, along with praise choruses projected on a screen, are forms of new media that have created discussion among church members about the value of holding on to the *old* and resisting the *new*.

One way to think about this (and any other) paradigm shift from an old way of seeing things to a new way is through the comparison to illusions. Consider this common picture:

What do you see? Does it help if we tell you it's a picture of a woman? What if we tell you it's a picture of two different women, depending on how you look at it? Sometimes at first glance we only can see or understand things one way, like the Pharisees and their understanding of the law. Jesus was offering a new perspective, a shift in viewpoint. Appendix A contains additional illusions that offer two ways of seeing something from one picture.

Relating to the Story

Understanding Jesus' use of the wineskins metaphor helps us look at change, specifically paradigmatic change that has happened and is happening. In the following chapters, we will explore several more Scripture passages in which we believe such change is at work. However, we need look no further than our present day to realize that we, as Christ followers, may be in the midst of a paradigm shift of faith and practice in the church today.

Phyllis Tickle, in her book *The Great Emergence*, quoting Anglican Bishop Mark Dyer, suggests that about every 500 years the church has undergone a significant change. She refers to these periods of change as "rummage sales" and states that we are in the midst of such a period today.[4] Tickle identifies former 500-year rummage sales as The Great Reformation (Oct. 31, 1517), The Great Schism (1054—Greek Orthodox and Roman Catholic), the leadership and influence of Gregory the Great (540–590—following the fall of Rome and start of the Dark Ages), and the Crucifixion of Christ, which led to the birth of the Church at Pentecost.

I (Dan) despise rummage sales, but it seems to be my fate in ministry to have served congregations that used them for fundraisers. Here's my view on how they work. People bring their junk, their cast-offs, the stuff they want to get rid of (rummage) to the church and clutter it up. A committee spends an inordinate amount of time sorting through it all and arranging the rummage for others to peruse. Then, on the day of the sale, folks come with an eagerness to riffle through other people's junk, finding prizes they simply cannot live without and paying pennies on the dollar to haul it away. But there always is more rummage left over at the end of the sale—as if it multiplies all day long. This means that the committee, already worn out from their week's long work of sorting, now will haul off the remaining refuse to a thrift store, or the dump, so that the church can be free of clutter. It always seems to me we would have been better off to just each kick in a hundred dollars and fund whatever project, event, or trip we were endeavoring to support.

But, I must admit, all I am seeing is the hard work and mess of the sale. From a balcony view it may be that rummage sales accomplish more than one first thinks. Over the course of a day, a week, or longer, rummage—that which is *old* and worn out—is removed, making room for the *new*. This then creates space to rediscover what remains in a new and vibrant manner.

This, we think, is Tickle's analogy of the rummage sale when it comes to the church. It's Jesus' new wine in new wineskins message. There comes a time when a shift needs to be made and change embraced. It seems like we are living in one of these times.

According to Tickle, rummage sales create upheaval and change with three consistent results or corollary events: a new and more vital form of faith emerges; the organized expression of faith until that time is reconstituted into a purer and less ossified expression of its former self; and faith spreads when the overly established form is broken up.[5] Consider the Reformation as an example: the Protestant branch of Christianity emerged with vitality; the Roman Catholic Church experienced its own counter-reformation; and the gospel spread because of both occurrences.

Reflection Questions

As you consider the changes in your ministry and congregational life today, how does this metaphor of a 500-year rummage sale resonate with your thinking? Where might we see evidence of the three results of a rummage sale type of change in the greater church today? Where are you facing, and adapting to, this kind of new wine/new wineskins change in your life and ministry context?

No matter how you responded to the above questions, you are not facing this change alone. Remember (from the Introduction) that we all tend to react to change as though we are in it alone, but we are not. Others in your congregation and other congregations and leaders are facing this same type of paradigm shift change today. Jesus' words about new wine and new wineskins are as applicable to us today as they were to his contemporary audience of religious leaders. Just as his audience consisted of persons who were at various readiness levels for Jesus' message, so too is the audience or congregation among whom you lead, worship, and live your daily practices of faith.

The Bell Curve of Change

Because people are at different levels of readiness for change, we feel it is helpful to share the following "bell curve of change" with you. This diagram found on page 13 and description come from the work of Merton Strommen, who describes five groupings of people when it comes to acceptance of change (or new paradigms).[6] The number in parentheses indicates the percentage usually present in any group:

1. **Innovators:** adventuresome; eager to try new ideas; often found outside official leadership circles (2.5%)
2. **Early Adopters:** respected by peers; persons with whom others check; frequently in leadership roles; often have more education (13.5%)
3. **Early Majority:** sometimes called "middle adopters"; seldom hold leadership positions, but adopt ideas sooner than average; deliberate in decision making (need to hear all sides of the issue) (34%)
4. **Late Majority:** approach change with skepticism and caution; do not agree to innovation until most others in the group have; may require pressure from peers to adopt (34%)
5. **Resisters:** sometimes called "laggards"; last ones in system to adopt (if they do); usually comprise a significant number of people who, though not leaders, can make themselves heard; tend to be least-educated and least-exposed to new ideas; suspicious of change agents; want to "hold the line" (16%).

The Bell Curve of Change

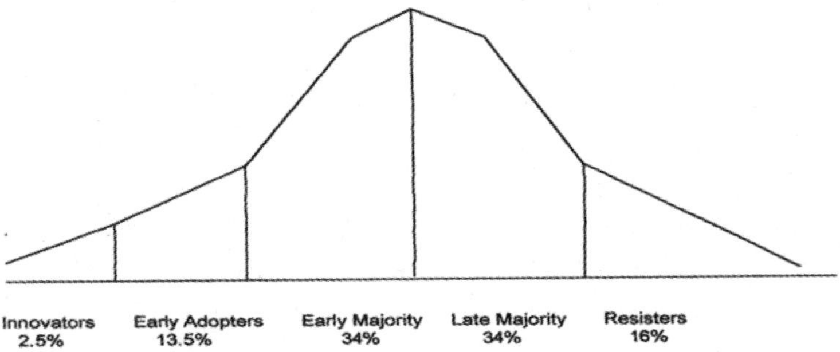

(Strommen, Merton P. The Innovative Church. Augsburg Fortress, 1997. p. 29)

Let's take Strommen's work and try to apply it to the Scripture passage from Luke 5:33-39. When you consider the people involved in this narrative (Jesus, John's disciples, Jesus' disciples, the religious leaders), where might you locate each group in the Bell Curve? Who were the Innovators? The Early Adopters? The Early Majority? The Late Majority? The Resisters?

Reflection Questions

Where do you often find yourself on this Bell Curve when it comes to facing change? Who comes to mind from your ministry as you consider the above groupings of people and how they embrace, or do not embrace, change?

Leading change is as much an art as it is a leadership science. We do well to be cognizant of the many personality types we lead, as well as to develop self-awareness when it comes to our own response to change. But, lest you be too discouraged, we would leave you with these more hopeful thoughts from the field of change theory. Consider these statistics: When just 5% of a group adopts the change, that change is embedded in the group. When just 20% adopt the change, change becomes unstoppable.[7] This is not to say that the change will occur overnight or be easy to adapt to and implement. It is to suggest that once a paradigm shift has taken hold, it will continue to move toward fulfillment. Once you've seen not just the older woman in the picture (page 9), but also the younger woman, you will not go back to seeing only one.

What will be your role as a leader in helping that movement go forward? As leaders who are trying to help persons come to grips with and embrace a paradigm shift of change, we would do well to ask ourselves the following questions:

a) How much opposition is present within the group to this change? How does this factor into my leadership approach? Who do I need to spend extra time with to help understand the change we are facing?

b) Of all the voices, which ones should guide us? Remember the loudest voice may not always equal the most discerning voice. Who am I listening to the most? How am I using my own voice?

c) Leading change requires a great expenditure of energy. Where will I invest my emotional energy in leading? How will I be replenished to be able to lead again?

If it is true that we are in one of those 500-year rummage sales as the church, then those of us who lead in ministry today will likely spend our entire lifetime helping the church through the change. Does that thought excite you or threaten you? If you are the type of person who must know what the change will eventually look like, you may be very frustrated. If, however, you can trust that God will see us through the change, you can enjoy the challenge and the journey. Which will you choose? What we hope to discover in these chapters is how such great paradigm shifts of faith occurred without persons "throwing out the baby with the bath water!"

Questions for Group Discussion or Personal Reflection

1. Which statement, idea, or example about change mentioned in this chapter would you most like to discuss? (Or which statement, idea, or example in this chapter would be the one you would mark with a yellow highlighter? Why?)

2. As you consider the narrative account found in Luke 5, and the five typical responses to change identified in Strommen's Bell

Curve of Change, where would you locate each of the participants in the story?

3. Where do you find yourself most of the time when it comes to change? Which group do you most often fall into? Who comes to mind in your congregation or ministry as an Innovator, an Early Adopter, etc.? Why?

4. Which of Jesus' metaphors (new wine and wineskins or cloth sewed to patch an old garment) do you most resonate with as it concerns change and your life and leadership experience? Share why this metaphor connects with you.

5. As one who leads or participates in change, what questions does this chapter cause you to ask yourself regarding your leadership or participation in your ministry context today?

6. Can you think of any ministry paradigm shifts today that might appear to be "throwing out the baby with the bath water"?

Notes

1. John Kotter, *Leading Change* (Boston, MA: Harvard Business School Press, 1996), 30.

2. To illustrate how persons of Jesus' day would have been familiar with rabbinical teaching using fermented and unfermented wine in old and new containers, we draw the reader's attention to the following quotes: Rabbi Yosi bar Judah of Kefar ha-Bavli said: "He who learns from the young, what is he like? He is like one who eats unripe grapes and drinks wine fresh from his wine press. But he who learns from the aged, what is he like? He is like one who eats ripe grapes and drinks old wine." Rabbi Meir used to say: "Do not look at the flask but at what is in it; there may be a new flask that is full of old wine and an old flask that does not even have new wine in it." See https://www.myjewishlearning.com/article/pirkei-avot-ethics-of-the-fathers-chapter-4/, accessed December 11, 2018.

3. Strong's Concordance, "3820 palaios." Biblehub.com. http://biblehub.com/greek/3820.htm, accessed December 11, 2018.

4. Phyllis Tickle, *The Great Emergence: How Christianity Is Changing and Why* (Grand Rapids, MI: Baker Books, 2012), 16.

5. Tickle, 17.

6. Merton Strommen. *The Innovative Church* (Minneapolis, MN: Augsburg Fortress Press, 1997), 29.

7. Strommen, 29.

CHAPTER TWO

Incarnation

John 1:1-9; 14-18

Leaders are now beginning to discover organic approaches that fit living organisms. Leadership, in this world, is more about "who you are," art and craft, and processes for the faith community. The conversation has moved more to leaders than leadership, more to processes than programs, more to what's natural than manufactured, and more to what's lasting than the quick fix.[1]

Scripture Encounter

2In the beginning was the Word, and the Word was with God, and the Word was God. 3He was in the beginning with God. 3All things came into being through him, and without him not one thing came into being. What has come into being 4in him was life, and the life was the light of all people. 5The light shines in the darkness, and the darkness did not overcome it.

6There was a man sent from God, whose name was John. 7He came as a witness to testify to the light, so that all might believe through him. 8He himself was not the light, but he came to testify to the light. 9The true light, which enlightens everyone, was coming into the world . . .

14And the Word became flesh and lived among us, and we have seen his glory, the glory as of a father's only son, full of grace and truth. 15(John testified to him and cried out, "This was he of whom I said, 'He who comes after me ranks ahead of me because he was before me.'") 16From his fullness we have all received, grace upon grace. 17The law indeed was given through Moses; grace and truth came through Jesus Christ. 18No one has ever seen God. It is God the only Son, who is close to the Father's heart, who has made him known.

Relating to the Story

One of the best illustrations of change that we can think of, as it relates to life and ministry today, is the change in mediums of communication that are readily available and in use. When I (Dan) stop to think about how I communicate with congregational participants today versus the mid 1980s, when I began in ministry, I am amazed by how many new mediums are being utilized. Back in the day (the '80s), one used the phone (a land line), written mediums (letters, cards, a newsletter), and face-to-face conversation. Today the variety of mediums has increased exponentially. Still, there is the phone (more often a mobile smart phone than a land line). There are many different written mediums, (texting, instant message, email, social media, blogs, websites, and the old school handwritten or print publications). Face-to-face encounters are still very much a part of ministry (thank goodness), but might happen via FaceTime, Skype, GoToMeeting, or through some other video-driven technology. Each Sunday I preach not only to a gathered, live congregation, but also to a number of persons who join us via live streaming or who watch a recorded video of the service posted to our website. And, in my sermon preparation, I have the choice of reading the biblical text and commentary resources in hard print or online, as well as making use of a few podcasts that are dedicated to the support of preaching. It's a whole new world when it comes to communication!

Having so many choices in communication requires discernment. Before communicating with congregants, one must first determine which medium will be most effective in reaching them. Do they prefer a text, instant message, email, or phone call? Which is more apt to get their attention? Given the reason behind the communication, which medium is more appropriate for the sharing of this particular message or encounter? All of this makes Marshall McLuhan's famous quote, "The medium is the message,"[2] ever more profound and yet perplexing for the would-be communicator in ministry and life today.

The Scripture in Context

Communication mediums have always varied and changed over time. We see this in the ways God's message is shared in the Scriptures. The story of faith has been carried forward by both oral and written mediums, in multiple genres and voices. Prophets often spoke, wrote, and even acted out the message they shared. Preachers engaged in various rhetorical techniques as God's message was proclaimed. Apostles wrote letters and gave sermons, as well as shared interpersonal exchanges. The Bible is filled with many different kinds of written communication (history, prophecy, wisdom, psalms, gospel, epistle, and apocalyptic). God has always used, and continues to use, a variety of communication mediums. Some changes have been subtle, others more abrupt.

By far the most significant change in medium used to share the message of God occurred with the birth of Christ. In this case, the medium truly did become the message as God introduced incarnation, the Word becoming flesh and dwelling among us. Hebrews 1:1-2 summarizes this change in medium well: "Long ago God spoke to our ancestors in many and various ways by the prophets, but in these last days he has spoken to us by a Son whom he appointed heir of all things, through whom he also created the worlds."

In some ways this change was discontinuous with humanity's prior experience. God's message had previously been shared by a spokesperson like Moses or Elijah. Now it was being shared face to face through Jesus. Often, God had been perceived as distant or remote—accessible only through an intermediary or in the temple. Now God was present in the very person of the Christ, who came as Immanuel, "God with us." The disciples, the religious leaders, and the common people had no prior experience with this kind of up-close, intimate, in-the-flesh encounter with God. This was a radical paradigm shift.

In other ways this change, as it is described in the prologue of John's Gospel, was the continuation of what God had been up to from the beginning. John makes use of a contemporary term and concept to describe the incarnation: "logos" or "Word." William Herzog II suggests that the Greek word "logos" was well-known at the time of John's writing:

> The term logos had a long and storied history before it appeared in the Fourth Gospel. It was a term used by the Stoics to refer to the principle of reason that governs the universe, while Philo spoke of its creative power (named God) and its royal power (named Lord). The rabbis related logos to Torah, and logos also came to be associated with wisdom (*Sophia* in Greek and *hokma* in Hebrew). John uses logos to express a most astounding Christology, 'and the Word became flesh and dwelled in our midst, full of grace and truth.'"[3]

This use of a familiar term, repurposed in some fashion to describe the incarnation, gave John's audience a reference point on the importance of the Word as the ultimate (divine) source of power and reason. They would have been curious to hear and know more, especially about what he meant by the Word becoming flesh.

John also is building on an Old Testament understanding of "the word of God," or *dabar* in Hebrew,[4] to connect the logos to an ongoing expectation of God's message coming to humanity. Now, however, the message was not limited to the agency of a prophet but spoken directly from "God with us"—the ultimate revelation of God's self.

The Christology shared by John is echoed by the writer of Hebrews in 1:1-2 (as quoted at left), and by Paul in Colossians 1:15-17.

> [15]He is the image of the invisible God, the firstborn of all creation; [16]for in him all things in heaven and on earth were created, things visible and invisible . . . all things have been created

> through him and for him. [17]He himself is before all things and in him all things hold together.[5] (Colossians 1:15-17)

In the prologue to his Gospel, John (1:1-2) establishes that the logos was with God from the beginning: "In the beginning was the Word, and the Word was with God, and the Word was God. He was in the beginning with God."

By establishing the continuity of the logos from the beginning, John, Paul, and the writer of Hebrews demonstrate God's long and enduring engagement with humanity (and creation), now being understood and experienced in a new and changed fashion—incarnation. John's prologue, with all its poetic grace, culminates in the fourteenth verse, which says: "And the Word became flesh and lived among us" (John 1:14) or, as Eugene Peterson paraphrases, "The Word became flesh and blood and moved into the neighborhood" (MSG).

Relating to the Story

As we consider this paradigm shift—God's using a new medium (incarnation) to connect with creation—it may be helpful to note both its "continuous" and "discontinuous" characteristics, terms used today to help leaders and congregations understand and work through different types of change they may be facing.

Continuous change, sometimes also referred to as incremental change, is change that is tied to past experience. In working through this type of change, we simply are making an adjustment in something we've had prior experience with and want to improve. For example, a congregation may have a history of engagement in its community through local mission but feel the need to improve those connections by revisiting community needs and partnerships. Such a process of evaluation might lead to a reinvestment in local mission in a more efficient or effective way. This is continuous change.

Discontinuous change is change for which we have no prior experience or reference point. It is change of a completely new direction or orientation, outside our expertise and prior knowledge. Many of the challenges that congregations face today are of a discontinuous nature. For example, how do we engage in faith formation and discipleship with children, families, and adults whose patterns of attendance and participation are radically different from prior generations?[6] Traditional ongoing weekly delivery systems like Sunday School may not be the answer. New and different forms of engaging a congregation may be called for today.

An incremental response to this concern might be to offer a new class or program designed to win the attention and participation of our target audience. This would likely be a facility-based and program-driven delivery of content. A more discontinuous and adaptive approach, allowing for the complexity of life today, might be to explore other mediums of delivery and engagement that are not facility-based or even program-driven. Interactive blogs, use of social media, self-selected small groups with online and 24–7 available content for download and use could be one such response. Having a small-group experience at a ballgame or soccer field for a face-to-face encounter between travel games or deploying a minister of discipleship incarnationally to the venues where younger generations may be gathering (ball fields, pubs, or neighborhood pool) might be another. Such ministries may be discontinuous with a congregation's experience and require a new alignment of priorities and resources, but they are consistent with the mission of discipleship.

In introducing such change, however, a leader might do well to take a cue from what we've discussed in the prologue of John. While John introduced a new medium of revelation, the logos or Word made flesh, he was careful to tie that medium to God's ongoing engagement with creation. The logos was a new and discontinuous expression of an ongoing or continuous desire on God's part to relate to and share communion with creation.[7]

Reflection Question

How are you connecting the need for change with the ongoing message of God's love and concern for people as you address new challenges that you face in ministry leadership?

I (Dan) was leading a workshop on worship planning a few years ago for a gathering of churches when the topic of change in worship came to the surface. One of the participants in the workshop, an elderly man, spoke up rather forcefully. "I hate drums!" he said. I had to wonder where this rant might be taking us. The man continued, "I hate drums, but I love my grandson. My grandson goes to the worship service where there are drums. Because I love my grandson, I also go to that worship service." I could not have scripted a better illustration of change that day. This grandfather helped us all connect the love of God through the love of a grandparent for a grandson as having greater value than a particular medium of worship music.

Even when the methods of change are discontinuous with our prior experience, we can often find a continuous message of God's grace that gives permission for creative thinking and experimentation in methodology. This may lead us to a more incarnational expression of ministry.

In the above paragraphs, we have used additional terms that merit further exploration as they relate to leading change. Such terms as "incarnational," "complexity," and "adaptive" are commonplace today in the greater landscape of congregational and organizational change. We refer the reader to Appendix B where terms and types of change are more fully defined and illustrated.

The Scripture in Context

In John 1:6-7 we read: "There was a man sent from God, whose name was John. He came as a witness to testify to the light, so that all might believe through him." John the Baptist was God's change agent, the proclaimer of a new and discontinuous medium of revelation about to publicly come on stage. He, John the Baptist, came to announce the change. He came to prepare the way for the change that would be fulfilled in Jesus, the Word made flesh. John's role was significant in leading change.

On the Bell Curve of Change, which we talked about in chapter one, John the Baptist would be an innovator. He was that person in your congregation who says, "I've got an idea." Or, more than likely, this one goes forward with an idea, asking forgiveness rather than permission for its implementation. You all know that person, don't you?

John is the last in the line of Old Testament prophets. He is the one to announce the paradigm shift that is coming. Like a present-day public relations director, he comes promoting a change that is about to take place in a product line.

As is true of most innovators, John is viewed by people with curiosity. He draws large crowds in part because of his eccentricities, but more because of his message (see Matthew 3:1-6). Not everyone in the crowd is on board with the call for change that he introduces (see John 1:19-28). John was something of a polarizing figure. You either liked him or didn't. The religious leaders of his day, whom his call for change threatened, did not appreciate John's ministry or message, but the masses who came out to the Jordan River in droves responded to his call to repentance and baptism. This signaled a readiness for change among the populace, even if they did not fully understand all that it would entail.

Relating to the Story

There is a role for change agents like John the Baptist in the work of leading change. As a leader, or group of leaders, who feel called to lead your church or ministry organization through change, you will need to initially assume this prophetic role. It's about creating awareness and understanding through drawing attention to the need for change. Failure to establish these early steps (awareness and understanding) in the change adoption process will likely sink any lasting efforts in the introduction of change. (Note: In chapter four we will further discuss this process for leading change.)

John describes himself, quoting the prophet Isaiah, as "the voice of one crying out in the wilderness" (see John 1:23 and Isaiah 40:3). Often, this is an apt description for change agents for whom calling a long-established organization toward change can be isolating and lonely work. Remember how many will resist change at all cost? As many as 16%, according to Strommen's Bell Curve of Change.[8]

We would do well to learn from God's implementation plan for a major change: using John the Baptist to introduce the incarnation. John's work prior to Jesus' public ministry was critical to paving the way for Jesus.

As we write this chapter, our congregation, the First Baptist Church of Columbus, Indiana, is in the middle of a change process. I (Dan) have served as senior pastor here for nearly ten years. I came into a stable, healthy congregational system that had known incremental and continuous change over its history. I am blessed to have had predecessors who served long tenured pastorates (Bill for thirteen years and my immediate predecessor for eleven years), and who paved the way for me to enjoy a similar longevity. For the initial several years of my pastorate, we continued on a trajectory of incremental change that allowed the church to hold steady and even increase in worship attendance and participation. However, just a few years ago, I began to notice that both of those measures were showing some decline. We, like a lot of mainline congregations today, are an aging body of believers. And we, like most congregations today, face the societal shifts and challenges today's lifestyles and rhythms of living bring to regular participation in congregational life.

Because I anticipated a need for change and had some conception of the trends and challenges facing congregations, I spent a lot of time in my early ministry here trying to build awareness and understanding of the challenges we face. I found myself taking up that prophetic voice, not unlike John the Baptist, and crying out. I utilized multiple mediums to share that message—sermons, Bible studies, newsletter articles, blog posts, leadership team meetings, and interpersonal conversations. It was tedious work. I felt like a broken record, but as we now have embarked on this journey into a more deliberate change process I see that it was vital work. I would counsel pastors and leaders not to overlook or dismiss this work. The rest of our story is yet to be lived, but without some John-the-Baptist-like paving of the way, you will not even get the opportunity to lead lasting or meaningful change.

Returning to the Story in Context

In John 1:16-17, the Gospel writer offers the following summary of the dramatic shift Jesus' incarnation brought to the world: "From his fullness we have all received, grace upon grace. The law indeed was given through Moses; grace and truth came through Jesus Christ."

This shift from law to grace is not only substantive: it is transformational. It carries both discontinuous and continuous elements. In the person of Jesus and his ministry, there was a freshness and palpably new approach to faith and God not previously found in the Pharisaical keeping of the law. We read and feel this shift in the Gospels through both Jesus' words and actions.

Jesus illustrated this transformational shift when he answered the lawyer who wanted to know what he had to do to inherit eternal life (Luke 10). Jesus tells him a story about a wounded man on the road from Jerusalem to Jericho who was robbed, beaten, left for dead, and in need of help. A priest and Levite were also traveling on that road, but they had their own religious reasons under the law to walk by on the other side. The dramatic contrast of introducing a Samaritan as the one who stops and shows compassion is what illuminates how Jesus' illustration is discontinuous from the Pharisees' teachings.

When the teachers of the law, the Pharisees, condemned Jesus' disciples for doing what was unlawful on the Sabbath (Matthew 12:1-13), Jesus asked them a question:

> "Suppose one of you has only one sheep and it falls into a pit on the sabbath; will you not lay hold of it and lift it out? How much more valuable is a human being than a sheep! So it is lawful to do good on the sabbath." Then he said to the man, "Stretch out your hand." He stretched it out and was restored, as sound as the other (Matthew 12:11–13).

Discontinuous change is not only seen in Jesus' teachings, but also in his actions. In Luke 17:11-19, Jesus heals ten lepers. We may be so familiar with stories like this one that we forget how drastic such an act was in its particular setting. There were laws defining lepers' place in society. They were expelled from participating and socializing. They were on the very outside, beyond the concern of anyone. Jesus' action demonstrates a drastic change in offering them the grace of healing.

In John 8, we see grace offered to the woman who was taken in the act of adultery. The men who were ready to fulfill the law by stoning her changed their minds when Jesus said, "Let anyone among you who is without sin be the first to throw a stone at her." Such teaching and actions of grace illustrate throughout Jesus' ministry the discontinuous change that he introduced.

However, though Jesus' ministry seemed discontinuous with the law in some ways, it really wasn't. He said he came "not to abolish the law, but to fulfill it" (Matthew 5:17). That fulfillment happened in the flesh through the person of Jesus (the logos)—God incarnate. No longer was God's means of speaking to the people just a set of laws; now it was heard in a human voice, presented in everyday teaching and storytelling, and exemplified in a life that could be studied and followed. Jesus' ministry took on a 3-D quality, rising up off the parchment into a life lived out amongst people. It was incarnational. God had pitched his tent right in the middle of the neighborhood. As John 1:18 says, "[Previously], no one has ever seen God. [But now] it is God the only Son, who is close to the Father's heart, who has made him known."

In our familiarity with this paradigm shift (law to grace, prophet to incarnation), we may not always appreciate just how radical the change was for people. God in the flesh, dwelling among us, was unlike anything experienced by humanity since creation.

Relating to the Story

A change many congregations are learning about and experimenting with today is anchored in this paradigm shift. Incarnational (also called missional) ministry has become a hot topic and trend in local congregations. It is built around the idea of living out the mission of God in one's life context. Incarnational ministry involves a change in focus from a program-driven church that calls persons to come from the neighborhood into the church for engagement (study, fellowship, worship, and service) to a call for persons to go beyond the walls of their church into the community in mission. It is incarnational in the sense that individuals become the flesh and blood examples of Christ's love to others whom they interact with on an ongoing and regular basis. It's a new wrinkle on pitching your tent in the neighborhood.

Churches are making incarnational movements into ministry in various ways and levels of engagement today. Some emergent church movements have embraced an incarnational understanding of ministry by having their leaders and members physically move into and live in neighborhoods where the church is located and shares ministry. In 2007, when I (Dan) and my family moved to Columbus, one of the things that factored into our decision to purchase a home was proximity to the church. I wanted to live in the same neighborhood as the church I served. We purchased a home about three blocks from the church. Now, over the course of time as we walk, run, cycle, and drive through the neighborhood, persons have come to know of our connection with First Baptist Church and the church's desire to share ministry with the neighborhood. In some small way, this is incarnational ministry.

Neighboring movements and emphases have taken root among churches in some cities today as congregations encourage their members to take Jesus' words literally and love their neighbors. By learning your neighbor's names and praying for them on a regular basis, you begin to become aware of the joys and concerns of their lives and respond to them. For example, when our neighbors lost their dog of eleven years, we stopped to talk with them about that loss and followed up with them during our evening walks. These are not programs for church growth, but efforts to be the hands and feet of Jesus in the neighborhood.[9]

In similar fashion, churches are establishing neighborhood or community gardens, opening their green space and facilities to be used by their neighbors, forming ministry partnerships with neighborhood schools and service organizations, and working to become intentionally aware of who their neighbors are and what their needs may be. As Pastor Jonathon Brooks of Canaan Community Church on Chicago's south side stated in an interview on "The Calling,"[10] a Christianity Today podcast on leadership, incarnational ministry is making the move to not just be a church *in* the neighborhood where members drive in on Sundays or other days to meet and then drive home. It's not just becoming a church *to* the neighborhood where at certain set hours the church opens to share a food bank, clothes closet, or children's ministry with its neighbors. Rather, it is the church becoming a church *for* the neighborhood, investing in relationships and learning the stories of its neighbors, praying for them, listening to them, and engaging with them in the common ground of life. This is an incarnational approach to ministry consistent with what Jesus modeled.

A key to understanding "incarnational" ministry is asking: Do we see the church we lead as an organization or organism? An organization is hierarchical and even mechanical in understanding and function, whereas an organism is a living system requiring organic leadership that allows for the system's participation. The quote from Robert Dale at the beginning of this chapter highlights leadership from an organic viewpoint. Leadership is more about "who you are, art and craft, and processes . . . than programs . . . more . . . what's natural than manufactured . . . what's lasting than the quick fix."[11]

In a living organism, change is constant. It is similar to a garden where things are always changing. Plants are growing, weeds are being pulled, produce is being harvested, soil is being worked, and the gardener is working in the middle of all that ongoing change. This is the role of the pastor or church leader today in the living, ever-changing organism of the church. We must move away from "plug and play" thinking that views a congregation as a machine in which we move parts in and out, to understanding our congregations as complex, adaptive systems that are alive. These organic and complex systems, if allowed and attuned to the Lord, often have the capacity for self-organization toward better health and outcomes.

Perhaps an example will help us understand this principle of self-organization. For several years the leadership at FBC Columbus had a goal of implementing a stronger young adult ministry. Multiple efforts went into this goal, including the calling of a staff member who would have ministry responsibilities with this demographic. These efforts included formation of a Sunday School class, a Facebook forum, occasional social gatherings, and strategic planning sessions with the young adults to get something off the ground in the name of young adult ministry. Over and over again the efforts fizzled, so we backed off and continued to encourage and support our young adults individually and invite them into the ongoing life of the church through worship, music, leadership, and mission. In the absence of forcing a complicated or even tactical approach to this perceived ministry need, young adults began to organize themselves. Initially they formed a group that participated in a community trivia night at one of the downtown eateries. This gave way to other social engagements and the eventual formation of an ongoing small-group ministry organized, planned, and led by the young adults. This is self-organization and emergent change at work.

Not every story, however, is that successful. Nor is every change that painless, even though it did take time to happen. Churches are complicated and complex systems, and many of the changes we face in congregational life today are far from simple. One leadership role within change is to help the congregation understand the type of change it faces. In Appendix B of this book you will find several types of change defined. We encourage you to take some time to review that list as you determine the types of change you are facing today in ministry.

As leaders we often fail to identify the type of change we are facing or tackling. We underestimate the challenge or we apply tactics more appropriate to another type of change than the one we are really dealing with. Many of the underlying changes churches need to face today are of a complex nature and go to the very core of their mission. Such change must be approached from a spiritual foundation, not merely a strategic or structural angle.

When, as a judicatory minister, I (Dan) consulted with congregations that were looking at making substantive change, I frequently shared the following formula with them:

Spirituality + Strategy + Structure = Transformation

It is important to work the formula in this order. Too often we start at the opposite end with structural change, then apply a strategy and ask God to bless it. That seldom works.

What types of change are you facing in your ministry context today? Think about this question from several different angles. The presenting issue may just be a surface change related to programming that reveals a deeper change issue that merits being addressed. How are you bringing your faith (spirituality) into dialogue with this change?

Conclusion

We want to leave you with a hopeful word as we wrap up this chapter on incarnation. We serve and worship an incredible God who has demonstrated God's love for us so thoroughly in the incarnation of Christ. This real promise of "God with us" should give us lasting hope. God is in the midst of God's people—God's church. If God is in the midst of God's people, as we, God's people, turn to the Lord and allow God's Spirit to work among us, our creativity is going to emerge and lead us forward, no matter the challenge.

Over our lifetimes we have witnessed incarnational ministry emerge again and again. We have personally experienced the refreshment of God in our lives and leadership, sometimes when things felt the driest or bleakest. Consider Bill's story:

I (Bill) look back on my retirement from pastoral ministry (when I became a hospice chaplain) as an example of change that moved me beyond the organizational, structured expectations out into an emergent relational ministry unlike anything I had experienced in my thirty-five years of pastoral ministry. At my retirement, I received a gift from the church of a painted watercolor portrait of me surrounded by a collage of each of the five church buildings where I had served. The portrait hangs in my room, and as I look at it over the years, I came to realize that it does not have a visual of my hospice years of relational ministry. That is significant, because I have concluded that those years were my most rewarding ones of ministry. They were years when the ministry was "outside the box" that was represented by the church building and the organization that established standards and expectations for me as the pastor. Hospice chaplaincy, though, was relational one-on-one sharing with others that solely focused on the spiritual needs of the ones who invited me into their lives. The church's organizational underlying agenda of membership, budget, and promotion were never part of the equation that focused only on spiritual needs. Those needs emerged, not from any organizational program or vision, but from the lives of the persons who invited me to journey with them as they confronted the experience of dying.

Just as I discovered the needs of hospice patients through a relationship with them, I pray that you also will discover the needs of others around you and be provided with new experiences of incarnational ministry.

Questions for Group Discussion or Personal Reflection

1. How many different communication mediums do you use in the average week? Which medium do you prefer? How do you determine which one to use when?

2. As you think about Jesus' incarnation, where are you able to see it as the continuation of God's love and message? How was it something very new?

3. What are examples of "continuous" and "discontinuous" change you face in your ministry context today?

4. How do you address new challenges you face in ministry leadership today and connect the need for change with the ongoing message of God's love and concern for people?

5. Can you identify any John-the-Baptist-like change agents in your congregation or ministry setting? What do they do around change that gives others permission to change?

6. Do you and the people with whom you serve Christ see the church more as an organization or organism? What are the implications for that when it comes to leading change?

7. What types of change do you face in your ministry context today? Think about this question from several different angles. The presenting issue may just be a surface change related to programming that really reveals a deeper change issue that merits being addressed.

Notes

1. Robert Dale, *Seeds for the Future: Growing Organic Leaders for Living Churches* (Danvers, MA: Lake Hickory Resources, 2005), 26.

2. Through his often-quoted famous words, "The medium is the message," Marshall McLuhan meant that "the form of a medium embeds itself in any message it would transmit or convey." https://en.wikipedia.org/wiki/The_medium_is_the_ message, accessed December 11, 2018.

3. William R. Herzog II, *Feasting on the Word, Year B, Volume 1,* edited by David L. Bartlett and Barbara Brown Taylor (Louisville: Westminster John Knox Press, 2008), 191.

4. See Dabar=YHWH meaning in the following website: http://www.abarimpublications.com/Meaning/Dabar.html#.WTSXclKZM0o, accessed December 11, 2018.

5. A more detailed study of the subject of Jesus in the Old Testament may be found in the book: *JESUS on Every Page: 10 Simple Ways to SEEK and FIND CHRIST in the Old Testament*, David Murray (Nashville: Thomas Nelson, 2013).

6. According to authors Jim Ozier and Fiona Haworth in their book *Clip In*, the average church participant today is present 1.2 times per month on a Sunday morning. Jim Ozier and Fiona Haworth, *Clip In: Risking Hospitality in Your Church* (Nashville: Abingdon Press, 2014), 102.

7. Richard Rohr writes that the Franciscan view of the incarnation was not God's Plan B, but Plan A all along. "Franciscan alternative orthodoxy emphasizes incarnation instead of redemption. For the Franciscans, Christmas is more significant than Easter. Christmas is already Easter! Since God became a human being, then it's good to be human, and we're already 'saved.'" We site this reference not to discount the significance or need for redemption, but to point out that in the heart of God the desire for communion with creation—including humankind—has never changed. It is important to tie change in ministry today to that unchanging desire. See Richard Rohr, *Franciscan Mysticism: I AM That Which I Am Seeking,* disc 3 (CAC:2012), CD, MP3 download.

8. See Merton Strommen's Bell Curve of Change in chapter one.

9. The following authors and books speak to incarnational ministry through neighborhood investment and neighboring ministries: Jay Pathak and Dave Runyan, *The Art of Neighboring: Building Genuine Relationships Right Outside*

*Your Door (*Grand Rapids, MI: Baker Books, 2012*);* Rick Rusaw and Brian Mavis, *The Neighborhood Church*: *Getting Better at What Jesus Said Matters Most* (Nashville: Thomas Nelson, 2016); David E. Fitch, *Faithful Presence: Seven Disciplines That Shape the Church for Mission* (Downers Grove, IL: Intervarsity Press, 2016); and C. Christopher Smith and John Pattison, *Slow Church: Cultivating Community in the Patient Way of Jesus* (Downers Grove, IL: Intervarsity Press, 2014).

10. "How a Trusted Pastor Can Transform a Community," *The Calling*, episode 2, April 27, 2016, Richard Clark, publisher and online editor. http://www.christianitytoday.com/ct/2016/april-web-only/how-trusted-pastor-can-transform-community.html, accessed December 11, 2018.

11. Dale, *Seeds for the Future*, 26.

CHAPTER THREE

Born Again

John 3:1-21; 7:7-51; 19:38-42

Every organization has the opportunity to honor relationship because every organization is made up of people.[1]

Scripture Encounter

[1]Now there was a Pharisee named Nicodemus, a leader of the Jews. [2]He
came to Jesus by night and said to him, "Rabbi, we know that you are a
teacher who has come from God; for no one can do these signs that you do
apart from the presence of God." [3]Jesus answered him, "Very truly, I tell
you, no one can see the kingdom of God without being born from above."
[4]Nicodemus said to him, "How can anyone be born after having grown
old? Can one enter a second time into the mother's womb and be born?"
[5]Jesus answered, "Very truly, I tell you, no one can enter the kingdom of
God without being born of water and Spirit. [6]What is born of the flesh is
flesh, and what is born of the Spirit is spirit. [7]Do not be astonished that I
said to you, 'You must be born from above.' [8]The wind blows where it
chooses, and you hear the sound of it, but you do not know where it comes
from or where it goes. So it is with everyone who is born of the Spirit."
[9]Nicodemus said to him, "How can these things be?" [10]Jesus answered him,
"Are you a teacher of Israel, and yet you do not understand these things?
. . . . [14]And just as Moses lifted up the serpent in the wilderness, so must the Son
of Man be lifted up, [15]that whoever believes in him may have eternal life. [16]"For
God so loved the world that he gave his only Son, so that everyone who believes
in him may not perish but may have eternal life" (John 3:1-10, 14-16).

The Scripture in Context

John 3:16 is the verse that makes this passage famous. If ever there was a well-known verse of Scripture repeatedly quoted yet often taken out of context, this is that verse. Many who love this verse and find it hopeful and meaningful might appreciate another understanding of it as one of the great paradigm shifts of faith. It is only when we study the verse within its scriptural context that we begin to fully comprehend the level of change that is being introduced.

How is it that you know John 3:16? How do most people learn of this verse today? In the 1970s and 1980s a man by the name of Rollen Fredrick Stewart, also known as Rock'n Rollen and Rainbow Man, began appearing at stadium events like football, baseball, or basketball games where he often wore a rainbow-colored wig and dressed in ways to draw attention to himself. He became a born-again Christian, kept the wig, and added a sign that more often than not simply read "John 3:16." He would seek out locations in stadiums sure to be in line with the television cameras and hold up that sign for all to see. He managed to appear in the 1977 NBA finals, the 1979 MLB All-Star game, at the Olympics, the Augusta National Golf Club, and the 1982 Indianapolis 500. Stewart's story took a tragic turn when he was arrested in 1992. He currently is serving three life sentences for hostage-taking.[2]

Perhaps it wasn't Stewart and his sign that first introduced you to John 3:16. Maybe it was a Bible memory emphasis from childhood, a plaque or wall hanging at your grandparents' home, or the familiarity that builds over time from exposure to hearing this oft-quoted verse of Scripture. It is a well-known verse, and it's all about change—change of paradigm-shifting implications.

In John 3:1-21, we read about an encounter Jesus has with a man named Nicodemus. This man was a Pharisee and "a leader of the Jews" (3:1), meaning a member of the ruling council called the Sanhedrin. The Sanhedrin was composed of seventy men, plus the high priest, with a membership that included chief priests, scribes, and elders. As the supreme council or court in ancient Israel, people looked to the Sanhedrin for answers as to how they were to live their faith. This council was the authority that set and enforced the rules for the Jews.

As a member of the council, Nicodemus put himself and his reputation at some risk in seeking out a conversation with Jesus. Thus, he came at night, under the cover of darkness. He also appeared to come on behalf of others. We speculate this to be true based on his opening words to Jesus: "Rabbi, *we* [plural] know that you are a teacher who has come from God; for no one can do these signs that you do apart from the presence of God" (John 3:2). It could be that Nicodemus was on a mission on behalf of the Sanhedrin, or perhaps, more likely, he represented a faction within that council. Whatever the case may be, as this story concerns change, Nicodemus represents a religious stream of Pharisaical Judaism steeped in tradition and an understanding of God's election of his people group. He is part of the official group that interprets and enforces the Law of Moses. He is the past. He is tradition. He is institutionalism. He is religion. Jesus, on the other hand, is something fresh and new. Jesus has a message that peaked Nicodemus's, and perhaps others', curiosity. And, as John sets up the story, Nicodemus comes at night under the cover of darkness to ask his secret questions.

Relating to the Story

When we seek to lead change, we face obstacles, some external to us, some internal, and some a mixture of both. For example, a congregation that wants to effect change in its community today around the growing opioid crisis will encounter external obstacles common in working to curb addiction. These might include the ready availability of prescription drugs (pain killers), a general public that is desperate for a means of escape from life's difficulties, and the problem of under-employment in the community. Each of these obstacles, external to the congregation, is part of the resistance to a fast path toward change in what is a complex societal concern.

In similar fashion, this same congregation may experience internal obstacles around this change initiative. Some leaders may feel such a focus is not a priority and that it diverts attention and resources away from other ministries. Other congregants may be uncomfortable with their church taking such a public lead in what is a current and messy social topic. These internal opinions and feelings can become obstacles to change as well.

Finally, a pastoral leader in this example may confront a mix of external and internal obstacles herself. Other professionals in the community working on the problem may resist her presence and questions at forums, or not understand how a faith community could be part of the solution to the crisis. At the same time, she may feel resistance from within the congregation as her priorities and use of time are questioned by those she serves with as pastor. Such a mixture of opposition (external and internal) may cause feelings of dissonance within the leader, steering her to back away from a change initiative for fear of rocking the boat too much, or even jeopardizing her employment that she would otherwise have led with passion.[3]

One of the most common obstacles to change that leaders face is the obstacle of the past. This obstacle can be both external and internal. We tend to call it by names like "tradition" or "heritage." These are terms that have an institutional ring to them and are rooted in the preservation of what has been. Please do not misunderstand; there is good in tradition and heritage. We both are thankful for the church traditions and denominational heritage from which we came. There is good in the past. Can't you look back at your past and find many things for which you are grateful?

But when the preservation of the past stands in the way of a clear and better future, that past, or our remembrance of it, can become an obstacle to change. We can end up serving the past, or what we feel it represents, as opposed to moving into the change of the present or future.

In my ministry career, I (Bill) have introduced numerous ideas for the church to consider that involved making drastic changes, and not all of them were accepted. Some were met with obstacles that had to do with tradition or heritage, where holding onto the past outweighed moving in a new direction.

One of those ideas was to change the constitution of the church from membership only by immersed baptized believers to an open membership where believers who had been baptized by another method (sprinkling or pouring) would be accepted in full membership as a way to welcome more people into the community. For me this issue grew out of my personal experience when I accepted a call to my first church out of seminary. My wife was reared in the Wesleyan Methodist Church. She was baptized as an infant by sprinkling and not by immersion but was told she would have to be immersed to become a member of this church. She did not want any controversy over the issue to interfere with my new ministry, so she consented although she strongly disagreed and expressed her opinion to the Senior Pastor and the Board of Deacons.

Many years later, in one of the churches I pastored, this issue was brought to my attention by a new woman in the community who visited our church and asked if she could come to my office and discuss membership. I was delighted to meet with her. Her story was that three years before, at age thirty-five while living on the East Coast, she became a Christian through the outreach ministry of a Presbyterian church and was baptized by sprinkling. She expressed her appreciation for the worship services and the welcome she had received while attending our church and wanted to know about the path toward membership.

The church's constitution very clearly stated the necessity of immersion for anyone wanting to become a member. I shared this with her, but said I would like to take her request to the Board of Deacons and communicate her desire and story; afterwards, she and I could meet again. I was hopeful that the board would be able to discern the uniqueness of an adult woman making the choice to accept Christ as her Savior and choosing to bear witness to that choice through baptism by sprinkling. I shared her story and intentionally noted the difference in her situation compared to a person who was baptized as an infant.

After discussing the matter, the board was overwhelmingly against the idea of making an exception. I then asked them if they would consider reviewing the issue with the church council and propose a plan to have the church study it in order to consider making a change in the constitution. They again opposed the suggestion. I then met with the woman, shared with her their decision, and explained my attempt to convince them otherwise. She thanked me, but never attended the church again.

I did not want to give up on the idea that the congregation needed to confront the issue, so I prepared a series of sermons dealing with faith, baptism, and membership, and asked members for feedback on those sermons. My sermon on baptism was titled, "Just add water." In part of that sermon, I used the woman's story. I was hoping to plant some seeds and get feedback to help gauge how much support there might be for the church to deal with this issue. I got no voluntary feedback, and when I brought it up with the church council, there was silence until someone said that it was a deacon matter about which they already had decided.

I began to realize that the culture of the church reflected the culture of the community in that change was very difficult, yet it was in that church that my suggestion about changing the constitution to allow women to have full participation was accepted. Because the members had been willing to study this issue for nearly a year and make that change, I felt they would be open to the baptism issue, but they were not. I was very disappointed but knew that the ministry we shared together was vibrant and exciting with many signs of growth, and I personally had to move beyond the baptism issue hoping that maybe I had planted the seed.

How do you interpret the above story as it concerns change and the obstacle of the past or tradition? Some might suggest that Baptist heritage and doctrine are norms that outweigh the welcome and inclusion of persons from other Christian faith backgrounds, even those with an adult or believer's testimony. Others would see the devotion to a constitutional requirement of membership as an obstacle to progress and to drawing the circle wider in the name of Christ. Still others may feel an internal wrestling within their own thoughts and feelings over such a matter. Though they may feel a tug towards change, they experience the pull of tradition. Obstacles always surface when we attempt to make changes.

Returning to the Scripture in Context

"Darkness" and "light" are more than descriptions of the time of day in John 3. These terms are used repeatedly in symbolic ways in John's Gospel. In John 1:5 we read, "The light shines in the darkness, and the darkness did not overcome it." In John 8:12 Jesus says of himself, "I am the light of the world. Whoever follows me shall never walk in darkness but shall have the light of life." In John 13:30, Judas leaves the table of the Last Supper and goes out. "And it was night." John seems to be using darkness here to suggest more than the time of day. When Jesus says in John 3:19, "light has come into the world, and people loved darkness rather than light because their deeds were evil," he is inviting Nicodemus to think about his message and their conversation in a much bigger framework. Nicodemus is in the dark regarding the teachings of Jesus, so he comes seeking clarification. He comes to the one who is the light of the world, and he is about to be enlightened.

Nicodemus addresses Jesus in a respectful tone, calling him "Rabbi" and acknowledging his connection with God (John 3:2). He has not come to pick a fight or engage in an argument. He genuinely is seeking to understand Jesus' message.

Jesus responds to Nicodemus's complimentary query by offering him a riddle about a new birth, speaking in symbolic language to describe a needed transformation. Nicodemus is blocked from understanding by his own literal engagement with the conversation: "How can one enter a second time into his mother's womb?" (John 3:4). Jesus pushes him further to reveal he speaks not of a rebirth of the flesh, but of the Spirit: "You must be born from above" (John 3:7).

This is one of those places in the Scriptures where, if we are long tenured in our faith, we may wonder what's taking Nicodemus so long to put things together. But we must remember the tradition and culture in which he has been trained and raised. He comes from a proud Jewish story and heritage, anchored in the Law of Moses. It is a law that he, as a Pharisee, would have dedicated his life to understanding and interpreting. He and his people find comfort and identity in being God's elect, the descendants of Abraham, Isaac, and Jacob, whom God has promised to bless and make into a mighty nation. His faith has a communal and corporate identity. His culture does as well. He would have been unfamiliar with the Western concepts of individualism and self that we, in this culture, espouse. The language of a "personal relationship with God" was not part of his first-century Jewish vernacular.

Look at how Jesus moves him along. Speaking with reference to himself and his own future, Jesus says, "Just as Moses lifted up the serpent in the wilderness, so must the Son of Man (a title Jesus uses for himself) be lifted up (a reference to the cross), that whoever believes in him may have eternal life" (John 3:14-15). Jesus has taken a story from the Exodus, a formative time in Israel's history when an impatient and rebellious people suffering amidst poisonous snakes were offered grace and mercy when they looked up to a pole that Moses was holding on which a bronze serpent was carved.[4] Those who looked upon the serpent were healed. Could it be that Jesus is using a story from the past to pull Nicodemus into a new and fresh understanding of God's present story? He is offering Nicodemus a new framework from which to understand his message and ministry. He is shining a new light upon the paradigm shift that introduces a personal redemptive faith element into God's greater message of love.

This is the context from which verse 16 emerges: "For God so loved the world that he gave his only Son, so that everyone who believes in him may not perish but have eternal life." What is required? Belief? Personal belief? What is promised? Life? Eternal life? This verse, emerging from Jesus' conversation with Nicodemus, confronts Nicodemus's old paradigm of belief, in which only an elect people were loved, to now proclaim God's love for the entire world. It confronts the old paradigm of faith through the keeping of the law with the invitation to faith through the trust of belief.

Nicodemus is asked to overcome obstacles in order to adopt this new understanding of faith. The external obstacles of the religious system and tradition in which he is a leader are present. Also, the internal obstacles of doubt and fear most likely raise caution in his thoughts and feelings. Every leader of change knows this wrestling match.[5]

I (Dan) would often see this wrestling match in my former work as a regional judicatory minister in congregations where change took root. It typically occurred within lay leaders who had a long history with the congregation. As they watched and experienced change in the church they loved, perhaps in worship or in the approach to discipleship, they would lament the loss of a tradition they had known. While it may have been exciting to see new faces in the congregation, drawn there because of a change in approach, faithful laity would confess to a sense of loss over what had been, as well as some mixed feelings that they were experiencing. They wrestled with external and internal obstacles to change.

Other Obstacles to Change

We already identified two general categories of obstacles to change: external and internal. Let's explore in more detail some specific obstacles leaders might encounter within each category and some keys to leading past those obstacles toward change.

We will begin with two external obstacles that leaders often run into when seeking to introduce change.[6] The first obstacle is what we might call "shifts in expectations" that are placed on leaders today. Leading is a challenge in the most tranquil of circumstances within congregations today. A good and involved leader continuously moves back and forth between people, teams, projects, and responsibilities. All of this is done in the public eye. When you add the layer of introducing or working toward change on top of the myriad of things already required, "challenging" may feel too soft a word. A word like "difficult" might be a better descriptor. One reason for this, external to the leader and change, is the erosion of trust that has taken place for public leaders in general, and for pastoral and congregational leaders specifically. Our modern-day culture has a general distrust for, and suspicion toward, those in authority. Too many leaders, in and outside the church, have fallen from favor and given the general population reason for adopting this shift. Each time pastors or congregational leaders are in the news for the wrong reasons (embezzlement, sexual misconduct, etc.) their behavior makes it that much harder for their colleague across town.

When you then introduce significant change, which in itself tends to surface emotion and anxiety, a leader can come under an even greater microscope of doubt and suspicion. People begin to question the motivation. Is there an ulterior motive? How is this change in the leader's best interest? It is not uncommon for those being asked to change to transfer their personal discomfort or dislike of the change to the leader whom they identify with that change.

There is only so much a leader can do to address this particular external obstacle. Leading with authenticity and openness is a good start. Being a person of impeccable integrity is without question a need in any public leadership role, most especially in the church. Taking time to know and love the people whom you lead, including those who are at times hard to love and do not appear to reciprocate any affection, is also important. In a word, it comes back to relationships. Good leaders, leaders who earn the right to lead change, know that relationships are key—building them and maintaining them. Mobilizing the right people to support the change initiative is far easier when one already has a solid relationship with those people.

Over-communicating one's reasons for leading the group into the change is an additional means by which to overcome the obstacle of shifting expectations that leaders face. As a leader you will always be steps ahead of those you lead in any change process. You have been thinking, praying, and strategizing about this change for some time. A common mistake even professional communicators often make is to discount the amount and frequency of communication needed to convince others of a needed change. Getting people's attention can be challenging. Utilization of multiple mediums to communicate (print, digital, social, sermons, interpersonal interaction, groups) is important when we consider persons' patterns of participation and listening in today's ministry settings.

Showing respect for one's context is also a means by which to overcome the external obstacle of distrust that leaders often face today. Many congregational members have invested years of energy, participation, leadership, and giving to their church. For these people, the relationship with their church borders on the sacred. Also, the church is often perceived as the one last steady rock in a world of vast change. Is it any wonder that change in churches is looked upon suspiciously?

By showing respect for an institution's past story, important chapters, and victories, a leader demonstrates not only respect but also reverence for the common foundation that those in the congregational system share and have inherited. Failure to demonstrate this respect and understanding of context and heritage will only reinforce inclinations of suspicion and distrust that may be simmering below the surface.

A second external obstacle many leaders of change will face is "organizational inertia." I (Dan) often say that organizations have a way of bending you to their will and culture. A pastor new to a church often has about a six-month window in which he or she sees the landscape of that congregation with fresh eyes. Beyond that window of time, the pastor begins to view things from an insider perspective. Organizations like stability and predictability. Resistance to change is simply part of the organization's method of maintaining that stability.

It is not uncommon for a congregation exploring significant change to start out with great energy and enthusiasm for that process. Persons will volunteer to be part of the leader team. Congregants will willingly participate in meetings and discussion forums. People are interested in what's going to happen, but usually, not too far into the process, the overwhelming nature of the work required to initiate the change hits the leaders. In addition, criticism and resistance (passive and aggressive) begin to surface as a direction for change is forecast and explored. All of this is part of how the congregational system reacts to change. Persons bring their own personal systemic tendencies (often learned in their family of origin) into the process. When a persistent and committed leader and leadership team is absent, the change might either be compromised or abandoned. Unfortunately, when this occurs, it seems like the next opportunity for change gets kicked that much further down the road because no one has the appetite to go through the painful and difficult process again soon.

How does one deal with congregational inertia? We will address this in more detail by discussing a process for leading change in chapter four. However, for now, we would like to suggest two things that may help a leader overcome this obstacle.[7]

One must remember that in leading change we are leading people. Leading change can generate a lot of talk about process, which helps us organize and plan how we move forward, but we move forward with people. We should be careful, therefore, to attack the problems that arise rather than the people we lead. We want to help people see that we are *for them* (pro people) even when we may not be 100% for their idea. We want to communicate that we love and respect those we lead, even when we may be frustrated by their behavior or words. We leaders would do well to take our frustrations to the Lord in prayer. Here's a good saying: "If you don't turn to God, you will turn on them!" No one wants to see that happen.

External obstacles to change (under the umbrella of congregational inertia) often present themselves through people. As stated above, however, it's the problem and not the person that we want to overcome. Here are four quick techniques for dealing with the problem and the person:

a. Believe the Best: Refuse to diminish or demonize one who has another viewpoint.

b. Empathize with Your Opponent: Put yourself in his or her shoes.

c. Wait a Day: A cooling-off period is usually not a bad idea in the volatile work of change.

d. Reply Relationally: This means face-to-face, or at least voice–to-voice (phone). Do not use a text or email!

If these external obstacles to change are not daunting enough, remember we also must often overcome internal hurdles in our leadership of change. Many leaders today lack the needed skills to navigate the choices of change we face in congregations.[8] This is an internal obstacle. Change that is complex and discontinuous with our prior knowledge or experience requires leaders who have the ability to adapt. Such adaptation is generally dependent upon the learning (sometimes unlearning) of particular leadership skills.

Most pastoral leaders trained in traditional seminary settings came into the pastorate equipped to think theologically, exegete a sermon, make a hospital call, or listen in a counseling session. Few of us were equipped to face the congregational changes that have become characteristic of this day. Continuing education, including ongoing reading in the field of change leadership, is one means by which such understanding and skill can be gained. Participation in denominational leadership and church transformation efforts via a cohort experience are other avenues for peer learning.[9] Use of a leadership coach or change consultant might be another means to confront this obstacle.

A more troubling internal obstacle that rears its head in leaders is the obstacle of ego. A realtor once told Dan and his wife that the clergy was the profession she found most difficult to work with in her efforts to help persons buy and sell homes. When asked why, she said it was because they were used to being in charge and telling everyone what to do. They did not listen well and were not very patient. Ouch! But when you stop to think about it, pastors do live a life and routine that can reinforce ego. Many other leaders do, as well.

The obstacle of ego can surface in different ways. It may manifest itself as the need to be in charge of everything. Tackling complex change may be more than one leader can manage himself or herself. Delegation and group ownership will become important elements in any change process. If a leader always has to be in charge, the probability of significant change taking root in the congregational system will be severely limited.

The need to be needed is another way ego manifests itself, often in pastoral leaders. This ego-related behavior gets reinforced when a congregant says things like, "I just knew you would come," or "I'm not sure what we would do without you." This need also gets in the way of leading collaboratively and sharing responsibility with others. If the pastor has to make every hospital call, be present at every meeting, and be involved in every decision, the church system will become co-dependent. Change will threaten this co-dependency, because it will require more from all.

Reflection Questions

As you consider your ministry context and the obstacles you may face when it comes to leading change, with which of the above obstacles did you most identify? Would you be willing to share that insight with another leader in your congregation? Such an accountable action might be a good first step toward facing the obstacle.

Returning to the Scripture in Context

Nicodemus reappears two additional times in John's Gospel. These appearances lead us to believe that he succeeded in adopting the paradigm shift Jesus introduced in their prior conversation. Let's look at the evidence that may suggest that Nicodemus was successful in overcoming the obstacles to the change he faced.

In John 7:45-52, Nicodemus participates in a discussion that the chief priests and Pharisees are having about Jesus. Jesus had been teaching in the public square, and his words caused a division among the people. Some were taken with his words and speculated that he must be a prophet or perhaps even the Messiah. Others, including the Pharisees, wanted him arrested, but the temple police did not make the arrest. When asked why, they reported, "Never has anyone spoken like this" (v. 46).

This prompted stout objection among the Pharisees and the question, "Has any one of the authorities or of the Pharisees believed in him?" (v. 48). They try to draw a distinction between the uneducated common people of the crowd and their own religious elite. It is here, however, that Nicodemus speaks up: "Our law does not judge people without first giving them a hearing to find out what they are doing, does it?" (v. 51).

Why would Nicodemus interject this word? Why risk exposing himself to the ridicule of his peers? Could it be that his earlier encounter with Jesus left him thinking? Was he on the road toward adopting this shift in faith? Was a new birth beginning to happen in him? We think it was.

His final appearance in John 19:38-42 solidifies our belief. Here, Nicodemus appears at Jesus' crucifixion alongside Joseph of

Arimathea, who is identified in the text as a secret disciple. While Joseph makes the request of Pilate to take Jesus' body for burial, we are told that Nicodemus brings the mixture of myrrh and aloes to anoint the body and prepare it for entombment. No longer is Nicodemus hiding his admiration for Jesus in the darkness of night. Now he is willing to join one who is called a disciple in the very public act of caring for Jesus' body.

We submit that Nicodemus underwent a paradigm shift of faith—that he was born again. It was a process in which he went from being a seeker to becoming a public defender, and finally a grieving anointer. A process of change and faith in which he determined he could overcome the external obstacles and trust Jesus made room in his thinking for both his Jewish understanding of faith and this new idea of being born again. Whatever external conflicts he may have wrestled with were reconciled when he adopted the change. Nicodemus's story, long revered for its part in the proclamation of the gospel, also should give us hope when it comes to change. He demonstrated the ability to adapt and embrace a change that led him to abundant life. Isn't that what we are all looking for?

Questions for Group Discussion or Individual Reflection

1. Try putting yourself in Nicodemus's situation. How would you have felt in approaching Jesus that night? What would you have hoped to gain from the conversation?

2. In this chapter we describe the obstacles to change that Nicodemus faces as both external and internal. What are some external obstacles to change that you face in your ministry context? What are some internal obstacles?

3. How do you interpret Bill's story about baptism and church membership as it concerns change and the obstacle of the past or tradition?

4. Where would you put Nicodemus on the Bell Curve of Change (see chapter one)? Why?

5. What new insight or discovery about change did this chapter help you make?

Notes

1. Gary V. Nelson and Peter M. Dickens, *Leading in Disorienting Times: Navigating Church and Organizational Change* (Duluth, GA: Chalice Press: TCP Books, 2015), 65.

2. http://articles.latimes.com/2008/may/19/sports/sp-crowe19, and https://en.wikipedia.org/wiki/Rollen_Stewart, accessed December 11, 2018.

3. One of the more common conversations Dan had with pastors as a regional judicatory minister around leading change in a congregational system included the confession that they would have led differently (more boldly) had their employment not been at risk.

4. See Numbers 21:1-10. Faced with the struggle of the wilderness, their past life in Egypt has taken on a revisionist history. Congregational leaders know this phenomenon as the "glory days" talk of those who long for the past, not always remembering its struggles and hardships.

5. Richard Rohr, *Falling Upward: A Spirituality for the Two Halves of Life* (San Francisco: Jossey-Bass, 2011), 11. Rohr writes about the obstacles religious leaders face in leading change:

"If change and growth are not *programmed into* your spirituality, if there are not serious warnings about the blinding nature of fear and fanaticism, your religion will *always* end up worshiping the status quo and protecting your present ego position and personal advantage—as if it were God! . . . This resistance to change is so common, in fact, that it is almost what we expect from religious people, who tend to love the past more than the future or the present."

6. The obstacles listed in this section are identified in the work of Nelson and Dickens, *Leading in Disorienting Times,* 10–15.

7. These ideas for overcoming the obstacles to change come out of the work of Nelson and Dickens, *Leading in Disorienting Times,* and Carey Nieuwhof, *Leading Change without Losing It: Five Strategies That Can Revolutionize How You Lead Change When Facing Opposition* (Cummings, GA: The reThink Group, Inc. 2012).

8. Nelson and Dickens, 14.

9. Many denominations and judicatories today offer leadership and/or congregational cohort experiences related to congregational change. The Nehemiah Network and Missional Church Learning Experience are two examples from within our American Baptist circles.

CHAPTER FOUR

Kingdom Manifesto

Matthew 5:13-20

Manifesto—"A written intention declaring the intentions, motives or views of its user."[1]

Scripture Encounter

13"You are the salt of the earth; but if salt has lost its taste, how can its saltiness
be restored? It is no longer good for anything, but is thrown out and trampled
under foot.

14"You are the light of the world. A city built on a hill cannot be hid. 15No one
after lighting a lamp puts it under the bushel basket, but on the lamp stand, and it
gives light to all in the house. 16In the same way, let your light shine before others,
so that they may see your good works and give glory to your Father in heaven.

17"Do not think that I have come to abolish the law or the prophets; I have
come not to abolish but to fulfill. 18For truly I tell you, until heaven and earth pass
away, not one letter, not one stroke of a letter, will pass from the law until all is
accomplished. 19Therefore, whoever breaks one of the least of these command-
ments, and teaches others to do the same, will be called least in the kingdom of
heaven; but whoever does them and teaches them will be called great in the king-
dom of heaven. 20For I tell you, unless your righteousness exceeds that of the
scribes and Pharisees, you will never enter the kingdom of heaven.

Reflection Questions

Do you remember a time when one of your long-held beliefs or ways of understanding the world was challenged? Can you recall how that process led you to adopt a new way of understanding or a new belief? Do you remember how that felt? Were you defensive? Perhaps you were a bit disoriented or confused. How long did it take for you to come to that new understanding? Was it a process over some time, or did it happen right away for you? How did it happen?

Straddling a Threshold of Change

I (Bill) have led two churches through the process of changing their long-standing traditional policies of the role of women in the church. Each of the church's constitutions, written 100 years earlier, still identified men as those who were to fill the major leadership roles. There were women who, out of the necessity to have someone qualified, were elected to the offices of financial secretary and treasurer. "Out of necessity" here meaning that there were no men who had the same amount of professional training in the field as the women. The culture in which the church existed was changing, and women were being schooled in professions that allowed them to enter the workforce as certified public accountants.

Since this door opened, I thought there was an opportunity to open it further by recommending that the church consider addressing the role of women in the church. The major leadership role that was male-dominated was the Deacon Board. The constitution included a Deaconess Board, which specified such duties as preparing the communion elements, washing the communion cups, and washing and ironing the communion tablecloth and napkins. I knew this was the major hurdle we would have to confront.

When I brought up the suggestion at the church council meeting that we consider this issue, I received positive feedback as well as some negative feedback from those who thought it was a bad idea because it might generate too much disapproval within the congregation. The council agreed that the Board of Deacons should discuss this matter and bring back a report. That was all that I hoped the council would do because it gave me the time and opportunity to prepare for further discussion of concerns at the next meeting. I was prepared to lead a discussion that allowed persons to share their views and reasons, knowing that both sides would be represented. After the discussions, I requested that the deacons consider not taking any vote on the matter but rather agree to have me lead six all-church meetings where the issue could be studied from a biblical perspective. They accepted. My plan was to use a six-VHS tape series led by Dr. David Scholer, a professor at Northern Seminary. The dates were set, and the sessions were well-attended. The biblical passages were presented and then discussed. I also preached on topics that enabled me to treat the need for change from a biblical perspective so that the total congregation was able to be aware of the importance of the issue. I knew that the final decision had the potential of creating division, but as we continued the process and prayed for God's leadership in it, I felt we were doing all we could to process such a change.

It took nine months for the process to reach the church for a vote. With all of the proper notifications met, the vote was taken following a Sunday morning worship service. A vote of 75% was needed to change the constitution. When all the votes were counted, the revision passed by just three votes. Some said to me on the way out of that meeting, "That close of a vote means nothing but trouble."

Two persons did leave the church because of the vote, but after a year of having men and women serve together, even those who were at first against it affirmed it. At our year-end training for the newly elected diaconate, one deacon who was against the change stood up and confessed, saying, "I was against it from the beginning, but now after a year together I wonder why we didn't do this years ago." I am blessed in my retirement years to be back worshipping in that church (Dan is the pastor) and to see women serving in all capacities of leadership.

As Bill's story illustrates, when we adopt change, or lead others in a change process, we often enter a time of liminality.[2] In liminal space, we are straddling a threshold. We have one foot in what has been (what we have believed) and one foot in what will be (a future belief yet to be fully adopted). This is an experience of displacement that occurs over a period of time.[3] Many congregations today experience liminality. As leaders committed to helping our congregations through change, we are called upon to help them move through the liminal space. We are called to lead them through a process of adopting change. In this chapter, we will explore one means of understanding that process in Jesus' teachings from the Sermon on the Mount (Matthew 5–7).

The Scripture in Context

Jesus preached and taught more about the kingdom of God or kingdom of heaven than any other topic.[4] The kingdom was the object of most of his parables, many of which begin with the phrase, "The kingdom of heaven (God) is like . . ." It was a topic he used to establish a new and different expectation among his listeners and followers. In his Sermon on the Mount, Jesus sets down some core principles and teachings that define this major paradigm shift of the kingdom. He gives us his kingdom manifesto, as it were, declaring his views and calling for a new understanding as those views intersect with old ways of thinking. We invite you to take a few moments now to read Jesus' sermon in Matthew 5–7 as we prepare to look at some of its core teachings and how they call for a shift in the ways that faith is viewed and practiced.

The Gospel of Matthew is written and shares Jesus' message with a primarily Jewish audience in mind. These are people living in their homeland, first-century Palestine, as a captive and governed nation under the rule of Rome. As an occupied nation, their experience of kingdom is very different from the days of King David or King Solomon. They long for deliverance from the oppression of Rome, and they often turn to the words of the prophets that promise a coming king and kingdom to stoke their hopes for the future.[5]

Within this greater Jewish community three major groups are mentioned in Scripture, each of which in its own way is attempting to realize and negotiate a future in response to Roman occupation. These groups are the Sadducees, the Pharisees, and the Zealots. They, along with the general population, constitute the audience to whom Jesus presents his kingdom manifesto. Here is a brief summation of each of these groups:

> The Sadducees mostly were members of the wealthy, conservative elite. They had opened their hearts to the secular world of Greek culture and commerce . . . Politically, they contented themselves with the way things were and resisted change—preferring instead to promote cordial relations with Rome. . . . The Pharisees, the largest group, mostly were middle-class Jews who emphasized the exact keeping of the law as it had been *interpreted by sages, elders, and rabbis*. Politically, they were ardent anti-Hellenists and anti-Romans. . . . From among the more politically radical of the Pharisees there came a new group called the Zealots, meaning "men of action."These were revolutionary patriots, who sought to overthrow the Roman regime by whatever means necessary.[6]

All three groups were living in a time of liminality, what Alan Roxburgh describes as "the conscious awareness that as a group (or individual) one's status, role, and sequence-sets in a society have been radically changed to the point where the group has now become largely invisible to the larger society in terms of these previously held sets."[7] This is to say that within the wider culture, dominated by Rome and imperial rule, the influence of these Jewish groups had become marginalized (perhaps with the exception of the Zealots who may always have functioned from the margins). While they (particularly the Sadducees and Pharisees) may have continued to hold a central role within the Jewish community, they held little or no sway over Rome and her governor. This was a radical shift in position and influence from the historical roles the groups had played.

The church in North America today finds herself similarly marginalized within the greater society. Unlike the days of Christendom when the church and our leaders were seen as central building blocks of a community, today life has displaced us to the periphery in our communities. Our position, like the groups described above, is one of liminality. Roxburgh suggests such liminal displacement has two common components: 1) An external event of change has happened or been thrust upon the group, leaving it outside its familiar frameworks and on the edge of chaos; 2) the inner response to the change is characterized by confusion or bewilderment, followed by depression and identity loss. This leaves the group asking, "How could this have happened?"[8] Have you ever heard or asked that question? Do you hear it asked in your church?

Relating to the Story

As previously stated, I (Dan) am in the midst of leading our congregation through a change process. As I write this chapter, a leadership task force working on the change has just shared its recommendations (its manifesto) for change with our church council. This came after a six-month process of listening meetings, garnering of information, study, and reflection. This process, I would argue, came about after years of communicating the need for change and the changing landscape of ministry today. The initial steps of building awareness and understanding were critical to gaining permission to move forward with our change process toward recommendations. However, as I watched the faces of our leadership team while these recommendations were shared and discussed, it once again struck me that change is hard. It's emotional. It's overwhelming. Even when we understand that it is needed, we can find ourselves thinking and perhaps even asking, "How could this have happened? How did we get here? Why does everything have to change?"

I also had to remind myself that the task force and I had been living with these recommendations for quite some time before we shared them with the church council. We were further down the road in our thinking and adoption of the changes being proposed, while the changes still were new to the ears of the others. We needed to back up and allow them the time and space to consider the information, process their questions and concerns, and come to their own understanding and adoption of the recommended changes. This is why leading change is often described as a process. It happens over time.

Even as we identify the need to approach change as process, let us share a further word of caution. Many of us have had the experience leading an organization or team through a linear change process. This works when the challenge being faced is predictable and the change incremental. Gilbert Rendle says that a linear change process has four steps: a) problem identification, b) alternative solutions (brainstorming), c) decision-making (choosing from alternatives), and d) implementation.[9] Sound familiar?

The change that congregations face today is not predictable or incremental but consists of adaptive challenges and discontinuous change that require a different leadership process. Rendle suggests that we view the process as chaotic.[10] Rather than view this process as linear, we might see it as a frenetic moving back and forth, up and down, to and fro between multiple leadership issues and tasks.

Several years ago, I (Dan) remember being in a large convention center with my family and my sister-in-law's family for a common meeting. Her son Ben, not more than three years old at the time, found the escalators of this facility fascinating, and he loved riding them up and down. He loved it so much that when it came time to leave, he resisted. In fact, he got away from his parents and onto the escalator and rode it up to the next floor. As one of them pursued him there, he got on the down escalator and started to descend. When the other parent stood at the bottom to catch him, he started climbing back up the down escalator toward the top. Eventually, his parents contained him, but it was a humorous episode to watch (since I was not his parent!).

This is what it's like to lead a group through complex adaptive change today. It's like moving up and down a set of steps, only they too are moving. (See Figure 1 below.) You advance from step one—creating awareness for the need to change—to step two—building understanding of the change being proposed through dialogue and discussion—and onward. As a leader, however, you often must go back to an earlier step, in order to companion someone who has not yet advanced to the same place in the process of change. This is the back and forth, or the up and down, of the chaotic change process.[11]

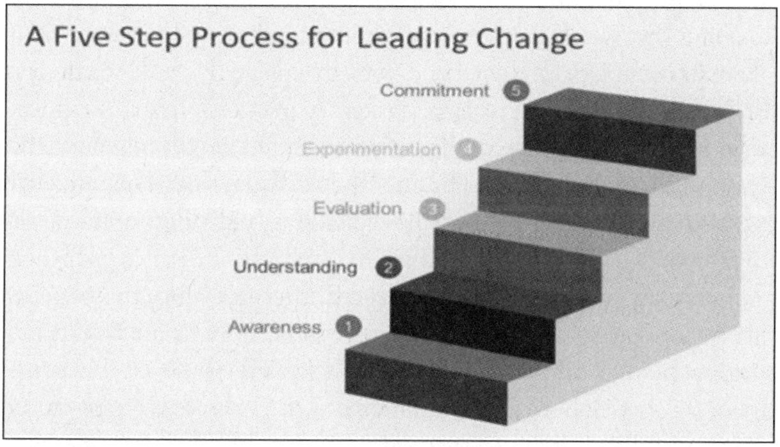

Reflection Questions

As you consider your own ministry context and whatever changes you may be facing today, where are you as a leader in the process? Which process have you been applying (linear or chaotic)? What step(s) are you working on? Where would you put those whom you are leading?

Returning to the Scripture in Context

As the people of Jesus' day lived in the disruptive environment of Roman occupation and hoped for a political or militaristic overturn of that reality, Jesus came bringing a different message. His kingdom manifesto represented a paradigm shift. He wasn't asking his listeners to follow him through change into what had been in David or Solomon's day, or even to what they may have envisioned might be—an independent Jewish state. He invited them into the chaos of a new and fuller understanding of kingdom. It was an understanding in which each of them was invited to play a role: to be salt and light (Matthew 5:13-14) in a way that the three groups identified above (Sadducees, Pharisees, and Zealots) had failed to do. The Zealots had determined to bear arms against Rome; the Pharisees closed the world out and worked harder at keeping the Torah; and the Sadducees tried to collude with their Roman occupiers. In these behaviors, they all had lost their saltiness or hidden their light under a basket. In contrast, Jesus' disciples, who lived by being salt and light, would bring kingdom values and ways of living into the community they called home. The influence of this new kingdom way or rule of living would be felt and known over time.

As his sermon was further delivered, Jesus took up the very law his opponents revered. His kingdom manifesto was not to destroy the law but to fulfill it (Matthew 5:17). Let's think about that statement as it relates to leading change. Often those who push for change in the church are met with resistance in the form of "slippery slope" thinking. Defenders of tradition and ritual will sound the warning that if we change one revered custom or practice, we are in danger of sliding down the slope on all that matters. Leaders of change would do well to note Jesus' approach with his critics. He upheld the message and meaning of the law, even as he introduced a new method for understanding it. When people come to see that a change in approach need not be a change in values or beliefs, change becomes more acceptable.

In Jesus' case, his proclamation was that the kingdom was present in his ministry and message. It was not just a future hope dependent on political or military overthrow: it was present now. What a shift in thinking! According to the preacher, however, it would require "righteousness" greater than that of the scribes and Pharisees to recognize and enter this kingdom (Matthew 5:20). Adopting the kingdom manifesto necessitated letting go of other pre-determined outcomes and becoming open to God's new thing. It required the willingness to follow Jesus into and through the chaos of a new understanding of kingdom.

Jesus used a recurring phrase in his sermon to anchor this change in viewpoint: "You've heard that it was said . . . but I say to you" (see Matthew 5:21 and repeated often in Matthew 5–7). It may be that the use of this phrase is to point to the interpretations of the law (what was "said" about it), advanced by the Pharisees. In this way Jesus may be making a distinction between what was written in the law, and what had been added to it through interpretation. Often it was this interpretation that created an additional burden for the people.

As an example, let's consider what was written in the law of the fifth commandment: "Honor your father and mother" (Exodus 20:12). In Mark 7:9-13 Jesus says,

> "You have a fine way of rejecting the commandment of God in order to keep the tradition! For Moses said, 'Honor your father and mother,' and 'Whoever speaks evil of father or mother must surely die.' But you say that if anyone tells father or mother, 'Whatever support you might have had from me is Corban' (that is, an offering to God)—then you no longer permit doing anything for a father or mother, thus making void the word of God through your tradition that you have handed on. And you do many things like this."

The interpretation (what was said) of the law in this respect superseded what was written, negating the intent of the law and misdirecting support from parents toward support of an institution.

In his sermon, Jesus confronts this kind of abuse of the law by using his phrase "but I tell you" to point individuals toward the root attitudes underneath the keeping of the law. For example, in Matthew 5:21 and following, Jesus reminds his listeners that the law said, "You shall not murder," but Jesus says don't even be angry with your brother or sister. Anger is the root cause, or attitude, that can accelerate to murder.

In like manner, the law said, "You shall not commit adultery" (Matthew 5:27). Jesus takes this to the root issue of lust, saying, "anyone who looks at a woman with lust has already committed adultery with her in his heart." This was a new understanding of kingdom-living, a shift in thinking and practice, reinforced throughout the Sermon on the Mount.

Jesus' kingdom manifesto teachings had more than personal implications for his audience. He did not just share a sermon about how we improve our own relationship with God. The common thread that ties all the points he makes in his sermon together and makes them important as kingdom standards is that all of them are about relationships.

For example, let us consider the impact that his teachings held for women of that day. In his remarks about adultery (5:27-30) and divorce (5:31-32), Jesus addresses how relationships within the kingdom, as well as the attitudes and behaviors that accompany them, must change to show respect for women. Mosaic Law stated that a woman was accorded an inferior legal status. She was considered the property of her husband (Exodus 21:3, 22). Divorce was a male prerogative (Deuteronmy 24:1-4). In fact, the Hillel school recognized even the most trifling cause as enough for divorce, something as simple as a wife burning her husband's food.[12] Also, it was common for Jewish religious leaders in their practice of prayer to thank God for three specific things: God thank you that 1) I am a Jew and not a Gentile, 2) that I am free and not a slave, and 3) that I am a man and NOT a woman.[13]

In his comments about divorce, Jesus states, "anyone who divorces his wife . . . causes her to commit adultery." This might be understood as his acknowledgment of the vulnerable state of women in that time. A woman was dependent on marriage and the economic security it afforded her and her children. Divorce would often cause a woman to seek the shelter and security of a next marriage, rendering her adulterous under the law. Jesus is once again addressing the foundational or root cause of the problem along with its consequences, and elevating the worth and value of women at the same time.

In Matthew 6, the midsection of Jesus' sermon, he continues this foundational look at the religious practices of the day and the significance of relationships. Almsgiving (vv. 1-4), prayer (vv. 5-15), fasting (vv. 16-18), and purity (vv. 19-34) are presented not just as external works of goodness, but with an eye toward the intention and attitudes behind them. Jesus' hope is that the kingdom will take root within those who give, pray, fast, and live a life of purity. These practices become natural outcomes of kingdom-living, and at the same time show value for the other. This was new and different thinking from a system that had reduced such practices to mere functions of law-keeping.

In Matthew 7, Jesus brings his manifesto to a close with warnings against judging others (vv. 1-5) and an admonition to treat others "as you would have them do to you," The Golden Rule (v. 12). He then shares a sequence of image-driven statements (narrow gate, wolves in sheep's clothing, bad and good fruit, wise and foolish builders) in the remainder of the chapter to reinforce that kingdom life involves choice, obedience, and commitment.

Relating to the Story

As always, Jesus' leadership in the Sermon on the Mount is noteworthy. As he introduces this major change in understanding the kingdom of heaven, he does so in ways we might implement for our change process. His teaching models an invitational quality that welcomes and invites others into relationship and process. He consistently helps us see the need to draw the circle wider to include those who often are left out, be that women (particularly in his day, but often yet today) or others who may find themselves on the margins when it comes to leadership and decision-making. His sermon also addresses those who oppose him and invites them into this new understanding of the kingdom. One of the ways we frequently set ourselves up for disappointment or failure when it comes to leading change is by not being inviting in the way that Jesus taught, and especially toward those who may disagree with us. Drawing the circle wider is a key part of any organizational change process. As we value relationships (even difficult ones), we learn to include, not exclude. Drawing the circle wider will make the work harder and probably lengthen the process, but it will more often result in a greater percentage of the group owning the change.

Also, it is interesting that Jesus uses a sermon to lead others into this new understanding of kingdom. This reminds us that, within faith communities, change, like almost all other issues, is at its root a spiritual issue and necessitates spiritual leadership. This may seem obvious, however, we have noticed how often faith leaders default to the latest organizational or business techniques when it comes to leading change instead of employing the common ground of faith, which is at the very center of the group's identity. While walking a congregation through change, a pastoral leader should not undervalue the role of preaching, prayer, and theological reflection on Scripture in his or her leadership. Not only are these natural and available avenues of leadership within the church—they are needed avenues.

I (Dan) was reminded of this as I walked with our congregation through our change process. Like many leaders who have an interest in the workings of organizational life, coupled with a capacity to think in a process manner, I led our team into a change process that initially undervalued the spiritual component. I assumed that because I had been praying about the issues and obstacles of change we were facing, others also were equipped to do so. In making that assumption, we jumped into focus group listening meetings designed around an appreciative inquiry method (see endnote 6 in chapter five). This was partnered with some reading, research, and continuing education for our team through available workshops and resources. Again, my understanding as the pastor was that all of this was unfolding simultaneously with a congregation that was in prayer about the matters at hand. But I was wrong, or at least I had miscalculated my own need to be more intentional and inviting of that spiritual prayer process.

After a couple of painful encounters with congregants who felt left out or overlooked in our process, and who pointed out the absence of an overt spiritual component, I began to rethink our approach. This led me to lead from a more centralized place as pastor and not just leadership coach. I called the congregation to prayer. We did this through a month-long prayer focus that involved three components: a) an individual prayer calendar resource that invited all participants into daily prayer, centered in a modified *lectio divina* approach (a type of reading and reflection on Scripture; see endnote 7 in chapter five for a fuller definition) and a named daily prayer need; b) congregational prayer gatherings that were lay and clergy-led, providing space for the voices of the people gathered in common prayer; and c) prayers in worship led by lay persons, giving voice to the prayers and language of the people, not just the pastors, as we continued further into our change process. I also developed a sermon series to address one of the stated goals of the church around change and shared that over the course of six Sundays. What I have learned from this experience is that it is vitally important to be intentional about the congregation seeing the need for change, first and foremost, as a spiritual matter. No one other than the pastor is in such a key position to call and give permission for this approach to change. Pastors, do not underestimate your spiritual leadership in the process of leading change.

Finally, we would point out that Jesus led his audience into this change of kingdom understanding through the use of repetition. His Sermon on the Mount was not his only mention of the kingdom. Jesus often spoke of the kingdom of heaven (God) as he shared parables or engaged in prolonged discourse with persons. He consistently modeled a kingdom that was present now in his ministry, while not yet fully realized. This repetitive reinforcement, shared in a direct and consistent manner, exposed persons to the paradigm shift of the kingdom and led them into their own process of adopting change over time. Jesus met his listeners on the escalator of change and traveled with them, inviting them to move from awareness to understanding and eventually all the way to commitment. His steady but patient leadership with his disciples helped them through their own experience of liminality.

A Non-Linear Process for Leading Change

In Figure 1 above, we have shared a set of stairs that helped us think about the progression of steps often found in a non-incremental change process. We would like to return to that illustration now. This information comes from the work of Alan Roxburgh and Fred Romanuk in their book, *The Missional Leader: Equipping Your Church to Reach a Changing World.*[14] The five-step change process they describe is illustrated in the figure on page 67. It is particularly helpful when people find themselves and their group in a place of liminality (straddling the threshold of what has been and what will be). Please take a moment to read through the process as it appears.

In our experience, while each step builds on the prior one, these are not steps one traverses in a linear or one-way direction. Remember Dan's nephew who was up and down the escalator, even climbing up while it was moving down? That's more the metaphor for working these steps. A leader often companions persons through awareness and understanding into evaluation and then does a retreat with that same person, remediating or helping the person unlearn a prior learning. In a group context, such as the church, no two persons ever seem to be in exactly the same place on the escalator, meaning a leader is back and forth, or up and down those steps, working alongside. Remember, too, that persons adopt change at different readiness levels. Some are innovators, others early adopters, and others middle adopters. This leaves the late adopters and, unfortunately, those who will likely never adopt. A leader has responsibility with all these groups and individuals and works to respect the rate at which they progress through the steps.

A Five-Step Process for Leading Change

To be able to lead during a time of liminality and adaptive challenge, leaders must be able to handle ambiguities of an uncertain environment. They must be able to lead others into those same ambiguities with a calmness and confidence that together they will discover the imagination of God that is going to bubble up in their midst.

Alan Roxburgh and Fred Romanuk in their work and writing (The Missional Leader) call for liminal leaders to walk their group through five steps described below:

Creating Awareness: Through intensive communication events, both one-on-one and in groups, leaders take people through dialogue and discussion about the need for missional transformation of the church (preaching, teaching, letters, books, conversation, etc.).

Building Understanding: The dialogue and discussion serve to bring thinking and feeling modes of understanding together into a coherent pattern of understanding.

Evaluation: What is currently happening in the congregation is evaluated in light of awareness and understanding.

Creating Experiments: People begin to identify actions that they believe will move them toward change. The critical word is action. People experiment through action.

Commitment: People commit to getting others involved in the process of moving through awareness to understanding, to evaluation, to experimentation, and finally to commitment.

It would be a mistake to think of this process as purely linear. Roxburgh suggests that you think of this a stairway of steps, but rather than moving linearly from one step to the next, the process is one of moving up and down the stairs to reinforce ownership of the steps and process as a whole.

Upon reaching the fourth step, creating experiments, a leader may spend considerable time and energy giving permission and encouragement for a group to engage in trial and error. Old messages will begin to creep in at this phase with language like, "We tried that once" or "I knew it wouldn't work." This makes leadership challenging, but one must adapt and become an encourager, motivator, coach, or counselor as the case may determine.

Celebrations, as well as bereavements, will need to be acknowledged in the change process. Change is difficult and creates loss, along with the complexity of feelings that go with that loss. A change leader will find himself or herself moving betwixt and between the roles of comforter, counselor, cheerleader, and coach and sometimes with little or no transition time to spare. All of this points to the importance of the leader's self-care and wellness. Leading change is not for the timid.

As I (Dan) consider the above comments, I cannot help but reflect on the real-life conversations I have in an ongoing fashion with persons in our congregation. Most weeks I am on this escalator of change, walking alongside someone who is responding in his or her own way. My leadership has heartened some who have been ready for change for some time, and it has frustrated others who may have felt that there wasn't a need for change, or that we were being too aggressive in our pursuit of it. I have offended colleagues, consoled co-workers, and tried to light a fire under those who were complacent. I have had to learn to manage my stress and find ways to step away from the work of leading change. I have endured long meetings, lunches, and coffees with people who needed to talk. I also have watched leaders grow, seen a spark ignite in one who found her voice, and witnessed hope return to others. I have become more energized in my leadership and ministry. Why? Because we pursue change that is worthy of pursuit. We address our situation of liminality. We believe that the kingdom is here among the people of God, ready for them to unleash their imagination, create experiments, and live into God's future.

Questions for Group Discussion or Individual Reflection

1. Where do you see evidence of liminality in your life or ministry context?

2. How do you feel about that liminality and change?

3. How does Jesus' kingdom manifesto and his example of leadership give you hope?

4. What step(s) are you currently occupying with your congregation on the escalator of change? Where are others on this escalator? What needs additional attention?

Notes

1. See http://www.merriam-webster.com/dictionary/manifesto, accessed December 11, 2018.

2. Liminality is an in-between space, often described as the initial steps of a transitional period. http://www.dictionary.com/browse/liminality, accessed December 11, 2018.

3. According to Richard Rohr, "Liminal space is always an experience of displacement in the hope of a new point of view." Richard Rohr, *Everything Belongs: The Gift of Contemplative Prayer* (New York: Crossroad Publishing Co., 2003), 49.

4. Texts like Matthew 3:1, 4:23, 13:11 and Luke 8:1 and 9:2 show the kingdom to be at the center of Jesus' teaching. In Matthew's Gospel, written to a primarily Jewish audience, the term "kingdom of heaven" is used, whereas the term "kingdom of God" is used in the other Gospels.

5. See Isaiah 9:6-7, Jeremiah 23:5-8, Ezekiel 37:22-25, all texts from prophets of the exilic period (another time of oppression in Israel's history) and their forecasts of a coming Davidic king or Messiah.

6. Andrew Cort, "Pharisees, Sadducees, Essenes, and Zealots." Beforeitsnews.com. http://beforeitsnews.com/spirit/2013/12/pharisees-sadducees-essenes-zealots-2483358.html, accessed December 11, 2018.

7. Alan Roxburgh, *The Missionary Congregation, Leadership, and Liminality* (Harrisburg, PA: Trinity Press, 1997), 24.

8. Roxburgh, *Missionary Congregation*, 26.

9. Gilbert R. Rendle, *Leading Change in the Congregation: Spiritual and Organizational Tools for Leaders* (Herndon, VA: The Alban Institute, 1998), 80.

10. Rendle, *Leading Change*, 82.

11. Alan Roxburgh and Fred Romanuk, *The Missional Leader: Equipping Your Church to Reach a Changing World* (San Francisco: Jossey-Bass, 2006), 84.

12. Manners & Customs: Divorce, "Divorce in Ancient Bible Times," Biblehistory .com. http://www.bible-history.com/links.php?cat=39&sub=760, accessed December 11, 2018.

13. Eugene Cho, "Thank God That I Am a Man and Not a Woman," Eugenecho.com. https://eugenecho.com/2011/06/09/thank-god-that-i-am-a-man-and-not-a-woman/, accessed December 11, 2018.

14. Roxburgh and Romamula, *The Missional Leader,* 105.

CHAPTER FIVE

Old and New Covenants

Jeremiah 31:31-34; Hebrews 9:11-14; 10:11-22

"People are not machines. They are living, changing, adapting organisms that come together in sometimes unpredictable ways to produce surprising results."[1]

Scripture Encounter

> 31The days are surely coming, says the LORD, when I will make a new
> covenant with the house of Israel and the house of Judah. 32It will not be
> like the covenant that I made with their ancestors when I took them by
> the hand to bring them out of the land of Egypt—a covenant that they
> broke, though I was their husband, says the LORD. 33But this is the
> covenant that I will make with the house of Israel after those days, says
> the LORD: I will put my law within them, and I will write it on their
> hearts; and I will be their God, and they shall be my people. 34No longer
> shall they teach one another, or say to each other, "Know the LORD," for
> they shall all know me, from the least of them to the greatest, says the
> LORD; for I will forgive their iniquity, and remember their sin no more
> (Jeremiah 31:31-34).

Relating to the Story

Have you ever been on the dissolution end of a covenant relationship? Our guess is that if you have spent any significant amount of time in leadership in the church, or as a member of a congregation, you have. This is an all-too-familiar situation in congregations today. A church member gets his feelings hurt or has a dispute about doctrine or the direction a ministry is headed and quits attending. Or a congregant hears about an exciting new ministry happening in a neighboring congregation and follows her "grass is greener" thinking there. When she is missed and contacted, the conversation can be awkward, defensive, and even angry. Sometimes the departing party may say something like, "It's nothing personal. We love you and the church; it's just time for a change." And just like that, in a day in which consumerism drives commitment more than covenant, the relationship dissolves. It can feel a lot like divorce and is almost always "personal" for those involved—many of whom never fully understand what happened.

Understanding Covenant

"Covenant" is not a word that surfaces very often in our day-to-day conversations, yet a great deal of life is lived out in covenant relationships. If you are married, you are in a covenant relationship. If you have a home mortgage or auto loan, you have a covenant agreement with your lender. If you live in a neighborhood that has a homeowners association (HOA), you are in a covenant relationship with the others who dwell nearby. If you pastor a church, you are in a covenant relationship with your congregation. If you are a member of a church, your church probably has a church covenant. Covenants determine commitments between parties. The commitment may be keeping wedding vows, promising to make installment payments, agreeing to abide by guidelines when it comes to the appearance and maintenance of your home and property, understandings of the pastor-people ministry partnership, or the mutual promising made by members of the same congregation.

Though the word "covenant" is not all that commonly used today, the concept is familiar to most of us. In fact, God chose covenant as a means of relating to humankind. Many of us may have encountered it in the Scriptures and in the mediums through which we study them—sermons, Sunday School classes, and small-group lessons—because the Bible is filled with the language of covenant, and it continues to be the principal way in which God interacts with us. However, the way in which this covenant between God and God's people has been understood has changed over time. One might even say there was a paradigm shift of understanding within the covenant between God and the people of God.

A covenant is a formal, solemn, binding agreement between two or more parties for the performance of some action.[2] A biblical covenant is an agreement, or mutual promise, between God and the people of God (Israel, the church, or an individual), in which each party assumes an obligation toward the other.[3] Because covenants involve at least two parties, they are relational in nature, built on living out a relationship of mutual agreement with prescribed or promised behaviors toward the other. Most church membership covenants, for example, spell out what is expected of those who enter into that understanding of relationship.[4]

Covenants have been part of civilization for a long time, a variety of which were existent in the ancient Near East. These included the Suzerainty—Vassal Covenants, a conditional form of covenant that often regulated the relationship between a king and his subjects. The king might offer land on which to live and work and the assurances of security for life in that kingdom (on that land). In return, the king expected his subjects to contribute (by work, taxation, or military service) to the upkeep of the kingdom. This was a conditional covenant agreement built on the promise, "If you do this, then I will do that."

Parity covenants were agreements in which both parties were bound by an oath. We see an example of this in the Jacob and Laban story in which Jacob agreed to work seven years for Laban's daughter's hand in marriage (Genesis 29). You may remember the agreement ultimately became a two-for-one deal, as both of Laban's daughters (Leah and Rachel) were married to Jacob, and he spent fourteen years in his father-in-law's service.

Patron covenants were agreements in which a superior party bound itself to the benefit of an inferior party. One might argue that in God's covenant with Abraham (Genesis 12, 18), God, the superior party, was voluntarily binding God's self for the benefit of Abraham and his descendants.

Promissory covenants were intended to guarantee (promise) a future action. In Jeremiah 34:8, we read that King Zedekiah issued a decree that slave-owners were obligated to free their slaves in a time of siege. This is an example of a promissory covenant.

Finally, Royal Grant covenants were unconditional agreements in which a king granted land or some other benefit to a loyal servant for faithful and exceptional service in return. Normally, this grant was perpetual and unconditional toward the primary party, but conditional to the heirs, so long as they continued in the loyalty of the father. The Davidic covenant in the Old Testament would be an example of a Royal Grant covenant.[5]

The Scripture in Context

In this chapter we want to examine several examples of biblical covenants, including many that fit the types listed above, as we trace how God's covenantal relationship with God's people changed over time. Also, we will look at how appreciation for a covenant approach to ministry can become an asset when working through change with a church.

The very first covenant in the Bible, found in the beginning of the Book of Genesis, records God's having given Adam and Eve all that they needed for a life in relationship with God and with each other. God also gave them instruction—a covenant of agreement between them—to "eat freely" of all but one tree, "the tree of the knowledge of good and evil" (Genesis 2:15-17). When they broke that covenant agreement, they were expelled from the garden, the broken covenant forever changing the human relationship with God.

Five major covenants follow in the Old Testament between God and God's people:

1. God's covenant with Noah and his family, which was expressed as a promise to never flood the earth again. This covenant was sealed with the sign of the rainbow (Genesis 9:8-17).

2. God's covenant with Abraham and Sarah contained a promise to make them and their descendants into a great nation through which all nations on earth would be blessed. However, it required them to travel to a new land, change their names, and live as a people who worshipped the Lord alone (Genesis 12:1-3).

3. God's covenant with Moses and the Hebrew people was built on the promise to make them a chosen and holy nation if they obeyed God's voice and kept the law (Exodus 19:5-6).

4. God's covenant with David was given to establish him and his descendants as kings and rulers of Judah and Israel (2 Samuel 7:12-17).

5. God's new covenant with the house of Israel, as given to Jeremiah, foretold the coming of the Messiah, changing the terms of covenant forever (Jeremiah 31:31-34).

Each of these covenants was meant to affirm God's relationship with Israel at a specific time in history. Each one built upon the prior covenant, and in each example, the people failed at keeping the conditions that were set forth. But God continued to show love and concern for them by starting again with a new agreement.

In Jeremiah 31:31 we read the announcement, via the prophet, of a "new covenant with the house of Israel and the house of Judah." This covenant announcement anticipated the major change in covenant understanding that would be brought forth by the Messiah, a covenant that would be written on the hearts of the people and result in the remission of their sin. Now the promise would have an internalized understanding or belief of faith (written on their hearts) and would not be dependent on an external behavior, such as an offering or sacrifice. Now the promise would be everlasting, or eternal, and not temporary with the need of repetitive action in order to renew the commitment. This represented a change in covenant living. God, through the Messiah, took action to establish a new covenant that would forever change the circumstances by which persons live. The New Testament (sometimes referred to as the New Covenant) is the record of this covenant understanding introduced through Jeremiah's prophecy. It tells the story of Christ who is at the center of the covenant with the church.

In Hebrews 9:11-14, this new covenant, given through Christ and his actions, is compared to the old sacrificial system of Israel. Whereas that system was dependent upon human actors (the high priest) in human structures (a tent/tabernacle or temple) offering animal sacrifices that had to be repeated, now Christ, our high priest who came from God's heavenly dwelling, offers himself, a perfect sacrifice, given once and for all. This establishes the new covenant and signifies a major paradigm shift—or change—in understanding of the covenant relationship between God and humanity. Now we are a people of this covenant, reaffirmed each time we share communion with Jesus' words, "This cup . . . is the *new covenant* in my blood" (Luke 22:20; 1 Corinthians 11:25). This covenant, while reaffirmed in communion, is lasting and does not need to be renegotiated or replaced by another. What Christ has done for us has both immediate and eternal implications when it comes to life. Our response to this gift of grace (through worship, service, witness) is part of how we keep the covenant that Jesus has established with us. Individually we keep it with Christ, and collectively we keep it with one another and with Christ. We are a covenant people.

In our faith communities, we affirm this covenant in the rites of worship, such as baptism, parent-infant dedication service, confirmation, wedding, and church membership—all expressions of covenant. Some of these rites are companioned by vows, or covenant promises, made between the parties involved (individual, congregation, and God). Culturally, we are conditioned to emphasize the individual nature of these acts. However, each act is communal as well. We make promises not just to God, but to one another for support and care, mutual prayer, and aid for couples in keeping their marriage vows, rearing their children in the faith, and growing in their baptismal identity. We enter into these covenant relationships as fellow pilgrims in faith, needing the faith community's partnership in our own practices of our faith. This should make breaking or dissolving such covenants much more difficult in practice than it often appears to be. Perhaps it is time we revisited the implications of our congregational covenants, including how we move through change.

Our celebrations of communion, or the Lord's Supper, may be our most frequent reminders and reaffirmations of the covenantal nature of our relationships. Each time we gather at the Lord's Table, we share this two-dimensional act of worship: the vertical dimension with God and the horizontal dimension with the community. The Lord's Supper is shared in remembrance and celebration of the new covenant given through Christ and God's ongoing pursuit of relationship with humanity.

Utilizing a Covenant Approach to Change

I (Dan) once had a conversation with a pastoral leader about leading change. He was serving a congregation that had made significant changes under his leadership over the last decade. He volunteered that when he and the elders of the church made a change, they did not advertise or announce it in advance; instead, it just happened, and they let the people discover and respond to it accordingly. He also revealed that his congregation was transient and tended to turn over in congregants every few years. I could not help but wonder if a contributing factor to this revolving-door phenomenon in the congregation wasn't just the transient nature of the community, but also the abrupt, hierarchical, and non-covenantal approach to change that was employed. This pastor was fortunate to serve in a community where exponential economic and population growth provides a ready supply of new faces.

We do not recommend such a hierarchical and autocratic approach to leading change. We understand that it is one method currently espoused in congregational life today, and that it does tend to fit some leadership styles and church governance models. But we have a hard time seeing how it honors a covenantal understanding of faith. We believe that change involving those who are in covenant relationship should honor such an understanding of the relationship. In other words, everyone should have the opportunity to understand and contribute to the change process. While this approach will require more time and effort, it also will result in a greater level of ownership and stability within the congregational system.

To illustrate this covenant approach to change, we will share a bit about our congregational polity and denominational affiliation. Both of us are ordained in, and serve with, the American Baptist Churches USA. Ours is a non-hierarchical denominational system built on a covenant of relationships. We are not the American Baptist Church but Churches. Each congregation is autonomous and locally governed while in a voluntary interdependent relationship with all the other churches. Each church enters into a covenant of relationships in order to be part of the denominational family. The purpose of the covenant, and the relationships it facilitates, is for mission and ministry. The covenant extends beyond local congregations to the various ministry entities that make up the denomination. In our case, these are the Office of the General Secretary (the primary governance office which facilitates the work of the Board of General Ministry), and three additional ministry organizations (International Ministries, The American Baptist Home Mission Societies, and the Ministers and Missionaries Benefit Board). In addition, each of these entities has covenanted with the other, with the local churches, with thirty-four regional bodies (ours being the American Baptist Churches of Indiana and Kentucky), and a few other auxiliary organizations in an agreement on matters of mission funding and distribution as well as denominational services, resourcing of congregations and ministries, and partnerships for ministry collaboration. When someone says, "It's messy to be an American Baptist," it is likely this web of covenant relationships to which he or she is referring. In a nonhierarchical system of governance, change of any kind, but especially major and discontinuous change, requires a renegotiation of the covenant relationships. One can understand the challenge and complexity of this work, which too often is seen as a roadblock to working toward needed change. However, when leaders resolve to work toward change through a covenantal understanding, the probability of their owning that change increases. If we give persons the opportunity to be part of the process of change, they will have a greater probability of embracing that change.

You may be part of a different type of congregational or denominational polity and find our American Baptist example a bit cumbersome. However, every local congregation at some level is a covenant body of believers. Persons have joined the church (formally or informally) because they agree with its mission, purpose, style of worship, or vision. They have found an affinity of common ground with, and benefit to, their personal expression of faith and discipleship. They are in a covenant relationship with one another and the Lord through their local congregation.

We suggest that when the time comes for you and your local body to initiate change (and you may be at that time already), instead of initiating a top-down change mandate in which persons have had little or no participation, that you create a process that honors the covenant nature of congregational life which may be more readily accepted and helpful in the long term. Both approaches to change will require leaders to expend great interpersonal and congregational energy and leadership capital. The question for you may be, Do I want to expend that energy and effort on the way toward a broader ownership of change or in response to a surprise change that may be less-than-enthusiastically received?

Returning to the Scripture in Context

We stated earlier that the new covenant, forecast in the words of Jeremiah (31:33) and fulfilled in the cross of Christ (Hebrews 10:14-18), represented a major change, or paradigm shift, for the people of God. This change was rooted in the primary understanding of the covenant being internalized (written on their hearts) for those who believed in Jesus, and once for all in the act of Christ Jesus' sacrifice. The writer of Hebrews captures this in stating, "And it is by God's will that we have been sanctified through the offering of the body of Jesus Christ once for all" (Hebrews 10:10).

This biblical writer wants his listeners to understand that the new covenant communities of faith, formed in response to the preaching and teaching of the Apostles, have their roots in the old covenant. The comparison the writer makes to Jesus' priestly identity with that of the human priests of temple sacrifice is one way in which he establishes both the continuity and adaptivity of this change (Hebrews 10:11-14). Why go to such lengths in making this comparison of Jesus' acts with those of the Jewish system?

The change for those who heard this teaching must have been extremely difficult because of the generations who had defined faithfulness offering sacrifices. For them to be convinced that they did not need to do anything because one person (Christ) had done it for them would have been difficult. This was the opposite of the law, which governed many prescribed duties of their lives.

We might compare this to the challenge persons in the church face in accepting change today. I (Bill) have talked to persons of Roman Catholic heritage who shared with me the strangeness of being given permission to eat meat on Friday, which became acceptable to do when the church changed its teaching. The prior external act of abstaining from meat one day a week had become embedded in these persons' religious DNA; as a result, many continue to this day to eat fish on Friday.

Those of us who were reared in Protestant faith communities also have our embedded traditions that feel sacred, and that, when changed, can destabilize our understanding and practice of faith. Let's consider the long-held tradition of holding a Sunday evening worship service, which has now gone by the wayside in most congregations. I (Bill) grew up in churches with a tradition of the Sunday evening service. The first church I attended after leaving seminary and being ordained had a Sunday evening service, and I thought that was the norm. I was called to that church as the Minister of Youth and began my ministry with the Baptist Youth Fellowship (BYF) that met each Sunday evening before the service. Later, in my first solo pastorate, I discovered that the Sunday evening service—which was devoted to youth ministry, and which I also was expected to lead—was a much more relaxed time, as well as a beneficial use of my gifts. However, over time, the evening service was discontinued. While I enjoyed it and missed aspects of it once it ended, I also must admit that I did not miss having to prepare two sermons every week.

During the time I served this congregation, I was called one day by a woman who was new to the community and was looking for a church. She asked me, "Is your church conservative or liberal?" She was stunned when I replied, "I don't know." She then asked, "Do you have a Sunday evening service?" I said, "No we don't." She said, "Well, then you're liberal." I replied, "I'd invite you to come and worship with us for three Sundays, and then you will be better prepared to make that determination." The woman did, and she remained with that congregation for many years until her death.

When we are asked to change the outward forms of our faith practice, we know it is difficult to do so. We are challenged at our very core when changes occur in the area of our sacred beliefs. That is how the audience of the writer of Hebrews must have felt. That is how many in our congregations feel today about the vast change that has encompassed ministry. It is also why keeping our covenantal understandings of faith in mind can be a helpful means by which to work through change.

An Example of a Covenant Approach to Change

As we at the FBC, Columbus, embarked on our own journey of significant change in 2017, I (Dan) knew that it was important to design a process that would involve the congregation. We had introduced changes along the way during my tenure as pastor, but as we came to the close of 2016, I felt the time was right to move toward a more adaptive response to the challenges we faced as a congregation. I began that year to build the case of change with our leadership group (church council) through a retreat exercise that I called "Taking a look in the mirror." We celebrated the successes and change we had realized already as a congregation, but acknowledged that additional challenges were presenting themselves for which we had not made adequate responses. Having participated in that exercise, our leadership team affirmed taking the same information to a congregational meeting to give more stakeholders an opportunity to reflect on the information.

In early 2017, having already introduced the reflection exercise and allowed persons time to sit with it, I came back to our church council with the recommendation that we intentionally enter into a change process that in time became known as our "revitalization" work. With the council's endorsement, I took that recommendation to our annual congregational meeting to get the members' blessing and announce the formation of a Revitalization Leadership Team that would shepherd the work forward.

Once this initial level of congregational ownership was established, the leadership team began to design a process of engagement that honored our congregational polity and understanding of covenant. This included the following steps:

1. A listening, focus-group phase facilitated by members of the task force that gave everyone in the congregation an opportunity to participate in a small group in which each one would respond to appreciative inquiry-style questions.[6] Data from this phase was carefully documented for later analysis. As pastor, I did not lead or attend the focus groups, wanting persons to have the freedom to respond without the encumbrance of my presence. I did, however, stay engaged with the leadership team throughout this phase of the project to encourage their hard work and stay abreast of developments.

2. As mentioned in chapter four, simultaneous with the rolling out of the focus group work, we invited the congregation into an intentional season of prayer. This was done through a prayer calendar and guide sent to each household, inviting the participants to reflect in a *lectio divina* style[7] on a Scripture passage each week for a month, and giving them a daily prayer focus pertinent to the work of change. We also introduced a sequence of four prayer gatherings, planned and led by a prayer team (different in make-up from the revitalization team) to call persons into corporate prayer times for the work at hand.

3. The revitalization team met and worked throughout this process by taking, collating, and categorizing the input gathered from the focus groups and prayer sessions. We looked for common themes, affirmations, concerns, and directions that were surfacing. Over time it became apparent that there were several streams or paths that might move our ministry forward. We named these "ministry pathways" and began to talk about potential recommendations that could be shared with both the church council and congregation.

4. The initial work, along with specific recommendations for change in the ministry pathways, was shared with our church council for review and input. Then the congregation met, not only to share the information but to hold table group discussions to invite response to the recommendations and to submit notes and comments to the leader team.

5. Communication was a key component throughout the first six months of the change process. We were determined to keep the congregation informed of the work through a variety of mediums, and as pastor I used my leadership capital on more than one occasion to draw persons to meetings and elicit their involvement in this important work.

6. A sequence of follow-up engagement gatherings ensued, each of them focused on a particular ministry pathway, with an effort to involve key stakeholders in that pathway, as well as anyone from the congregation who was interested. A result of this work was the formation of much smaller and more manageable task force groups that continued to move the pathway change initiatives along.

The results of this change initiative are ongoing as we write. However, we are pleased to see the level of participation and interest in the work that came about as a result of our having designed and implemented a process that honored our congregational polity and the covenant nature of the faith experience. A few additional thoughts merit mention at this juncture:

a) Use of new language: It was important in our work to use a recognizable name to identify the change toward which we were working. “Revitalization” became the term that worked for us. By utilizing this name—often and in multiple formats—we helped people begin to recognize it as the change work. “Revitalization” became a brand that gave permission for discussion, study, reflection, prayer, and talking together about all things new. A logo or symbol might accomplish the same thing for a congregation.

b) The spiritual nature of the work: As mentioned previously, it was important for us to acknowledge that the change work we shared was first and foremost a spiritual endeavor. This was not primarily about institutional survival or continuity; it was about faithfulness to the gospel. In particular, it was about reaching persons with the good news who are not currently followers of

Christ, or who have no faith community in which they are participants. Prayer, along with Scripture reflection, became keys to this work.

c) The strategic use of the pastoral office: Often when attending a ministry conference, the presenter will share with those laity or church staff members who are present, "You need to make sure your senior or lead pastor is on board." When it comes to leading change, this is so true. I (Dan) once again have discovered that there are times when the weight of the pastoral office can call and hold people together. I have been the pastor of this congregation for ten years, working together during this significant period of change. That longevity and track record gives me credibility that would have been lacking had we introduced this process in my first, second, or even fifth year. Pastors should be judicious in how they work alongside the change process with their congregations, for though they may fill multiple roles, such as consultant, coach, cheerleader, encourager, preacher, prophet, etc., they must never lose sight of the overall position of pastor and all that it represents; it is a unique position to be inhabited wisely. You who are pastors should consider using the mediums available to you, such as preaching, teaching, and leadership development. Also, it is important to be available to talk with, and respond to, parishioners. Change scares people, confuses them, and causes misunderstanding. Pastors who are leading the church through these waters will find themselves working hard to offer a pastoral presence along the way.

d) Patience and the willingness to involve others: You cannot do it all, you cannot do it alone, and you cannot have it all done tomorrow. Significant, complex, and adaptive change requires time. No one leader has all the answers or ideas. Teamwork is critical to imagination and success. Good, active listening is necessary for all who lead. Patience—giving the process time—is important also. You always will live in the tension of wanting to see things happen but needing to make sure you move at the pace and with the purpose that serves the process best. Gauging this is very much part of the art of leadership.

Benefits to the Covenant Approach to Change

In a covenant approach to change, we honor and listen to God, we honor and listen to one another, and we collectively respond, moving forward together. This approach gives a congregation perhaps its best chance of staying together while working through and adopting change. It requires more time and effort, and it requires a leader and leadership team with a clear understanding of, and a commitment to, the process. There will be ups and downs, victories and setbacks, all from which the team and congregation can learn, if they are willing. Some will not have the patience for the process or will resist the call for participation. Some may leave, but most will be thankful for a genuine effort that is respectful, measured, and focused.

God's covenant initiatives with Abraham, Moses, and David were defining movements in the history of God's people. The initiatives stretched those leaders and the people who followed them as they all took obedient steps to live into the covenant. Jesus' new covenant, introduced through his ministry with the disciples, had an equally stretching and formative component to it. As this new covenant was written on hearts, in fulfillment of Jeremiah's prophecy, those hearts became more and more pliable and obedient to the Lord.

We trace our history as the Church and as congregations to the establishment of the new covenant through Jesus. We see ourselves in the men and women who left all to follow him. We find hope in the record of how the church has adapted and changed over its many years of ministry. We believe it is going to continue to do so, globally and locally. We believe it will do so most successfully as it remains mindful of the covenant nature of faith.

Questions for Group Discussion and Individual Reflection

1. What types of covenant relationships are a part of your life?

2. How does your faith community acknowledge and celebrate its covenant relationships? What traditions or worship practices have you, or do you, utilize to emphasize being in covenant?

3. How do you respond to the covenant approach to change illustrated in this chapter? What makes sense to you about this approach to leading change? What do you find challenging about it?

4. As you have reviewed the different expressions of biblical covenant in this chapter and how they progressed toward the "new" covenant forecast by Jeremiah and made real in Jesus, what do you see as the key adaptive changes God introduced? Why were these important?

Notes

1. Gary V. Nelson and Peter M. Dickens, *Leading in Disorienting Times: Navigating Church and Organizational Change* (Duluth, GA: Chalice Press: TCP Books, 2015), 65.

2. See https://www.merriam-webster.com/dictionary/covenant, accessed December 11, 2018.

3. Kenneth Clark, *Kerygma: Discovering the Bible,* ed. Boyd Lien (Pittsburgh: The Kerygma Program, 1989), 63.

4. As an example, the Church Covenant of the First Baptist Church of Columbus, Indiana, is found in Appendix D.

5. In a 2014 blog, Dr. Claude Mariottini, Professor of Old Testament at Northern Seminary, identifies these five types of ancient Near Eastern covenants also found in the Old Testament. See https://claudemariottini.com/2014/10/03/the-diversity-of-gods-covenants/, accessed December 11, 2018.

6. Appreciative Inquiry, or AI, is a change management approach that focuses on what is working well, analyzing why it is working well, and then doing more of it. It is based on a way of asking questions that encourages positive thinking. See http://whatis.techtarget.com/definition/Appreciative-inquiry-AI, accessed December 11, 2018.

7. *Lectio Divina* is a Latin term that literally means "divine reading." It describes a way of reading the Scriptures in which the reader gradually lets go of his or her own thoughts and becomes open to what God is saying. This practice of Scripture engagement traditionally consists of four steps: read, reflect, respond, and rest. See http://ocarm.org/en/content/lectio/what-lectio-divina, accessed December 11, 2018.

CHAPTER SIX

Resurrection

Luke 24:1-49

Don't forget your role in the bigger story. God is in the business of raising the dead!

Scripture Encounter

13Now on that same day two of them were going to a village called Emmaus,
about seven miles from Jerusalem, 14and talking with each other about all these
things that had happened.
15While they were talking and discussing, Jesus himself came near and went
with them, 16but their eyes were kept from recognizing him. 17And he said to them,
"What are you discussing with each other while you walk along?" They stood
still, looking sad. 18Then one of them, whose name was Cleopas, answered him,
"Are you the only stranger in Jerusalem who does not know the things that have
taken place there in these days?" 19He asked them, "What things?" They replied,
"The things about Jesus of Nazareth, who was a prophet mighty in deed and
word before God and all the people, 20and how our chief priests and leaders hand-
ed him over to be condemned to death and crucified him. 21 But we had hoped
that he was the one to redeem Israel. Yes, and besides all this, it is now the third
day since these things took place. 22Moreover, some women of our group astound-
ed us. They were at the tomb early this morning, 23and when they did not find his
body there, they came back and told us that they had indeed seen a vision of
angels who said that he was alive" (Luke 24:13-23).

Relating to the Story

No matter the change issues you may be facing in your personal, vocational, ministry, or congregational life, it can be helpful to know that you are not the only one facing change today. In fact, as we stated in the introduction, and again in chapter one of this book, it is safe to assume that you are part of the larger phenomenon of change that confronts churches, leaders, and citizens alike. The realization that others face change, too, can offset the tendency we have to feel as though we are all alone when change confronts us. These feelings of isolation often cause a chain reaction in our thinking which goes something like this, "I don't have the resources (time, knowledge, money, skill, patience, etc.) to make this change." Or, "No one else understands how hard this is." Or, "I just want to give up, do nothing, and hope it will all go away."

Have you ever felt that way? Maybe you feel that way today or this week about some type of change, some paradigm shift that you are asked to address and participate in. Don't give up! Through the lessons in this chapter, allow us to encourage you to hang in there with the change(s) that may confront you as we take a look at the most foundational change, or paradigm shift, in all of Scripture and history: resurrection![1]

The Scripture in Context

Because of our beliefs and familiarity with the resurrection story, it is easy for those of us who are part of the Christ-following way to overlook the fact that not everyone in Jesus' day believed in resurrection—his or anyone else's. While some of the Jewish religious traditions taught that there was a life after death, others (namely, the Sadducees) did not believe in the resurrection or eternal life[2] (see Acts 23:8).

Furthermore, few persons directly experienced the resurrection of another person. The exception in Jesus' ministry would have been those who witnessed his raising of Lazarus (John 11).[3] There were other scriptural forerunners to this phenomenon, such as Elijah and the widow's son.[4] As a whole, however, and for the average person, death was a final and life-ending reality. We would argue that this is still true for many persons, including—sadly—some who have espoused belief in Christ, but for whom life on this earth—and not eternity—is valued above all.

As pastors, we have counseled and been present with those saints in Christ who may have quoted the assurance of verses like John 3:16 throughout their lifetime, yet, when confronted with death and life beyond, they are uncertain and afraid. To some extent this is natural. No matter how many sermons or classes you've sat through on the promises of eternity, your experience, when it's your turn to enter eternity, will be an entrance into a mystery of much that is unknown. Therefore, we understand the questions and uncertainty on some level, but we also would be among those who have espoused that death, when you are in Christ, is not the worst thing that can happen to you. As Christ followers, we are a people of the resurrected one. This same risen Christ has promised that we, too, can know eternal life (see John 11:25).

This way of thinking and speaking—such as a proclamation of faith—equates to the foundational, radical, and transformational change or paradigm shift represented in Jesus' resurrection. This shift is the cornerstone on which the Christian story and faith rests. To quote the Apostle Paul:

> Christ died for our sins in accordance with the Scriptures . . . he was buried . . . he was raised on the third day in accordance with the Scriptures . . . he appeared to Cephas, then to the twelve . . . If there is no resurrection of the dead, then Christ has not been raised; and if Christ has not been raised, then our proclamation has been in vain and your faith has been in vain (1 Corinthians 15:3-5, 13-14).

The accounts of Jesus' resurrection are found in each of the four Gospels, with Luke's version being one of the more detailed. Luke 24 begins with the early dawn discovery by a group of women that Jesus' tomb is empty. Having gone there to prepare the Lord's body for burial and final rest (Luke 23:55—24:3), the women are instead confronted by "two men in dazzling clothes" who ask them, "Why do you look for the living among the dead?" (vv. 4-5).

This must have been such a jolting question. Many of us have come to know it through the liturgy and music of Easter, but consider the question when it was first asked. What? The one we knew to be dead, whom we witnessed die, is alive? What do you mean, "look for the living among the dead?" A shift in thinking and belief has been introduced. Change is in the offing. Angelic messengers have once again broken in to announce what God is up to, and it is radical and transformational. Resurrection!

But we must remember that these were women in the first-century context of Judea, whose eyewitness testimony was easily dismissed and discredited because of their gender and the status society assigned to them. We can imagine the men, who upon hearing the report, considered it but "an idle tale" (v. 11).

Luke tells us (v. 12) that Peter went to have a look for himself, no doubt to verify the women's story (v. 12). He, too, found the tomb empty and was "amazed." But what does Peter do with this information? Verse twelve tells us, "he went home." Change of this magnitude is hard to accept and hard to integrate into your thinking, even when you were as close to Jesus as Peter. Rather than return to the group and corroborate the story of the women, Peter went home. Having a lot to think about, he chose to deal with this change alone.

The next section of Luke's resurrection narrative, and the one that we want to unpack in this chapter, concerns two travelers who have been in Jerusalem, who know of Jesus' death by crucifixion and have, themselves, heard the report of his resurrection. Luke's narrative invites us along as these two travelers walk to Emmaus and are unexpectedly joined by another—the risen Jesus himself.

Jesus and the Two Travelers

Luke's narrative places the Emmaus road story "on that same day"—what we've come to call Easter day (vv. 13ff). We assume these two men have been to Jerusalem for the Passover feast, a religious expectation of every Jewish male within reasonable distance of the city. Now they are making the seven-mile journey home.

As they walk, they are mulling over the events of the past days and "all these things that have happened" (v. 14). Perhaps they are in a state of shock or disbelief. It certainly appears as though grief and sorrow have overtaken them. Things have not turned out as they had expected, for "[They] had hoped [Jesus] was the one to redeem Israel" (v. 21).

As Bill has written in his book *Tears in a Bottle: Learning How to Grieve Well*, "We who read Luke's account know the story so well that we are tempted to rush to its resurrection conclusion and miss the circumstances of sorrow and grief that define the emotions of the disciples."[5]

The two travelers are privy to the reports of Jesus' empty tomb, but these reports appear only to have added to their confusion, and not to have released them to any hope of Jesus' resurrection, so on they walk (vv. 22-24). Are they ready to give up? Is their mindset one of quitting? We cannot be certain, but there is no denying that they are discouraged and disappointed with the events and outcomes of recent days. Things have not turned out as they had hoped. The change they were looking for through Jesus now seems to be impossible.

Relating to the Story

When we hope for change—any type of change, but especially large-scale, systemic change—we walk through fragile space. Changing a long-established system, such as a congregation, or the way a family interacts and relates with one another, or the rule of government (as appears to have been the hope for many of Jesus' day), is big change. It is often discontinuous versus incremental change. It is paradigm-shifting change.

Often, those who are involved in these types of change efforts will come to a place of frustration that leaves them wanting to throw up their hands and walk away. There will be days when quitting feels like the best or only option. We suggest that Emmaus road travelers may have been in that place, walking through one of those days. You very well may know what we are talking about as you contemplate the systemic kinds of change you would like to see come about in your life.

Carey Nieuwhof, in his book *Leading Change without Losing It*, shares the following five ways that we can avoid quitting when we are leading change and at the point of frustration.[6]

1. *Find friends*, local and elsewhere who will companion with you.
2. *Get some help*. Talk to a coach or counselor; don't be a lone ranger in ministry or leadership.
3. *Create an encouragement file*. Keep notes, emails, and messages from persons who encourage your leadership and work.
4. *Find something energizing to occupy your time off*, and don't focus on work/change 24/7.
5. *Develop a devotional life that has little to do with work.*

These five strategies have much to offer a leader who is slogging his or her way through the work of paradigm shift change. I (Dan) can especially relate to these strategies as they concern my own ministry leadership. I serve a congregation that finds itself needing to change in order to stay vibrant and vital for ministry today. Founded in 1852, we are a long-established mainline American Baptist church with an aging membership nucleus. I have been the senior pastor for ten years. As I got to know the church, I discovered that it was further down the congregational life cycle than I had first thought. Well past its prime years, and in danger of slipping past its mature ones when there would be the opportunity for redevelopment, the church was at what George Bullard describes as the "empty nest" or "retirement" stage, heading toward the final, declining aging stage.[7] See the graph on the next page.

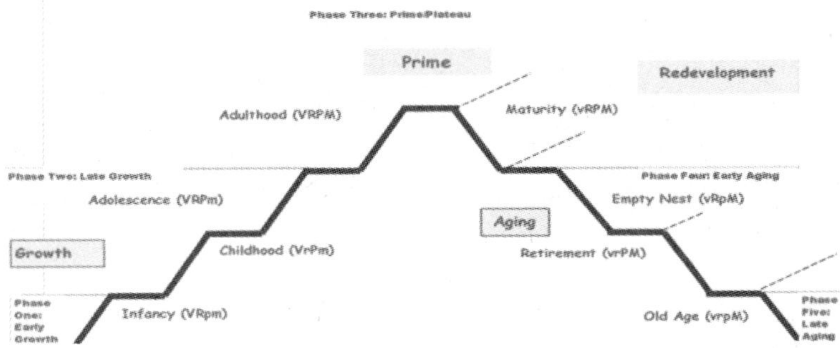

The Life Cycle and Stages of Congregational Development

With enthusiasm and effort, we were able to somewhat reverse the trend of decline during my first years of partnership with the congregation. Introducing incremental change through new language and focus seemed to cause the work of redevelopment to take root. But the aging nucleus has continued to age, and now it has become obvious to me and other congregational leaders that incremental change will not return us to a growth phase. Something more disruptive and discontinuous is required. Something more along the lines of a paradigm shift. Something like resurrection.

I share this story for two reasons. First, I think it is one that many congregations and leaders can relate to. Not all the stories of leadership today are wild successes of turnaround churches. Many, maybe most, are more like our story: one of a leader who strives to be faithful and help a congregation he loves to find its footing for a new day of ministry by facing the hard work of change; one of a congregation that wants to be vital and engaged in ministry and mission, but that also has deep respect and reverence for its heritage and past. It is not a Chicken Little "the sky is falling" story, for our congregation continues to share important and vital ministry in our community, as do many faithful congregations across the land today. Ours is a real-life story filled with the hardscrabble work of change.

My second reason for sharing this story is my hope that it will speak to that leader who is ready to throw in the towel. There have been many occasions when I was ready to quit. Some who were involved with our ministry but did not find it changing fast enough, or in the way that they desired, have quit and gone elsewhere.

In some ways, like those Emmaus road travelers, the frustrations of hoped-for outcomes not coming to fruition, or not happening as quickly as I had hoped, have been overwhelming. Pastoral and congregational leaders and those whom they lead need to acknowledge this. When it comes to change, the work that we engage with is long, difficult, and arduous. It is work for which there are few immediate rewards. Additionally, the work can become isolating; you feel like you are in it all alone. This is why Nieuwhof's five strategies to avoid quitting are so significant. Though not always aware of it, I have employed each of these strategies in my own leadership. Allow me to go through the list with some examples in hopes that it will encourage your leadership.

1. *Find friends*: My coauthor, Bill, has become a terrific friend who understands the challenges I face in leadership like no one else. Bill was the pastor of this same congregation two decades ago. It's unusual that a former pastor is able to come back to, and be such an integral part of, a congregation he once served. Bill sometimes refers to himself as my "Senior Associate." That sure works for me. I am blessed by his friendship, presence, and contributions.

At the same time, I also have friends who are not local, or directly involved in our congregation, who help to provide perspective and outside insight into the challenges we face. This, too, is helpful. It is important to avoid becoming a lone ranger in ministry or leadership.

2. *Get some help:* I'm a big believer in leadership coaching and have been blessed to have worked with a coach in the past. I also think there are times when having a counselor to talk with, formally or informally, is critical to one's mental health.

3. *Create an encouragement file:* I keep a file in my cabinet of notes and cards of encouragement that persons have sent to me over the years. I do not visit that file often, but it always has been helpful when I have done so. I also regularly journal to process my thinking. The ability to go back and review journal entries has helped me see that progress does come over time.

4. *Find something energizing to occupy your time off:* This is a big one for me. A few years ago I (Dan) took up the exercise hobby of cycling. My family gave me a bike for Father's Day, and I began to explore our city's trail system. I've since upgraded in bikes two times and I have become a pretty enthusiastic cyclist. This practice helped me lose thirty pounds, but more importantly, it has become a mental and physical health activity that brings balance to my life. Gardening, walking, and writing are a few of my other outside interests.

Twenty-seven years ago, I (Bill) discovered woodworking to be a creative and renewing experience. Not only was I able to design and make furniture for my family, but I discovered the joy in working on projects that I could step away from and feel the satisfaction of knowing that they were finished. This was especially gratifying because ministry so often goes from one connecting or continuing responsibility to another, often with no sense that anything is complete. Another benefit of my hobby is that it prepared me to enjoy my retirement.

5. *Develop a devotional life that has little to do with work:* This is a real challenge for those of us who regularly preach, teach, and communicate around Scripture. If we are not intentional with this practice, we will find that each time we sit with Scripture will become an opportunity to work up a sermon or lesson. I try to start most days with a prayer practice, rooted in Scripture, and other reading that is not geared toward producing a ministry resource. We challenge you to do the same. You will be better for it.

These same five practices that help one avoid quitting can be applied, we think, to the behavior of Jesus' disciples (the Emmaus road travelers, the women, and the eleven) in the resurrection story. Let's think about it together, starting at the beginning.

1. *Find friends*: In time, all of those who were eyewitnesses to the resurrected Jesus sought out the company of the other believers. The women went immediately to share news of the empty tomb. Peter, while he may have initially gone home, was found in the company of his fellow apostles as he met the risen Jesus again and again (Luke 24:36ff; Matthew 28:16ff; and John 21). And the Emmaus road travelers, after discovering the identity of their walking companion, "got up and returned to Jerusalem" to share this news with the others (Luke 24:33).

2. *Get some help:* One of the more fascinating aspects of the Emmaus road story is that the risen Jesus acts as the counselor or coach for the two travelers. He interprets the change they experience as they encounter him on the road (v. 27). He becomes their guide and companion, giving them insight into the Scriptures about him.

3. *Create an encouragement file:* The Gospels and the oral tradition behind them constitute such a record or file for the early church. It was as this story continued to be told and shared that belief in resurrection change took root.

4. *Find something energizing to occupy your time off:* One of the more interesting resurrection appearance stories of Jesus occurs in John 21 with Peter and the other disciples. Peter was determined to "go fishing" (John 21:3). Why? Did he need to provide for his family? Afterall, fishing was his livelihood. Or did he need a diversion? Did he need to get his mind off all that had happened and return to something he loves and finds fulfilling? We cannot be sure, but we speculate there is some of the latter at play.

Was the same true for the Emmaus road travelers? Was their trip a return home to the regular routine? Did it need to happen that day, or did they just need to get out of town and divert their energy and focus elsewhere? Diversions can be both healthy and unhealthy: those that are used to help us find space to process things are healthy, and those that are used to avoid things are unhealthy. Perhaps in the resurrection accounts we find a little of both.

5. *Develop a devotional life that has little to do with work:* From our place in history, it is difficult to imagine what the devotional life of Jesus' disciples must have been like. However, we assume that, as they spent time with Jesus, they learned the importance of this practice. We certainly see Jesus in his ministry often going off by himself to a quiet place away from the crowds to pray and commune with God (see Mark 1:35; Matthew 14:23; Luke 6:12). As their public profile increased, we have no doubt that Peter and the others needed to establish those same personal practices of faith and discipleship. How do you make sure that this is part of your routine?

Back to the Scripture in Context

It may be the intrigue of this Emmaus road story that so easily captures our attention as readers. The fact that "their eyes were kept from recognizing" Jesus allows him to companion them on this walk as both counselor and coach (v. 16). His question, "What are you discussing with each other?" catches them by surprise (v. 17). They cannot believe he, especially if he is coming from Jerusalem, is not aware of what has taken place there over the past few days. It would be the equivalent of a person in New York City the day after 9/11 overhearing persons talk of that terrible day's events in a restaurant, and then asking them what they are discussing. How could their new travel companion not know "the things that have taken place there [in Jerusalem] in these days" (v. 18)?

Jesus' follow-up question—"What things?"—more than suggesting he is unaware, is used to prompt their reflection on the things.[8] Here we see the craft of a skilled counselor drawing out the emotion from his client and feelings of the client's experience. Jesus invites them to put into words what they have witnessed, what they are feeling, and what conclusions they are making.

Jesus is acting as a grief counselor with two men who are mourning his death. Their response to his prompt is to allow not just the story of the last days to pour forth, but also the disappointment, confusion, and bewilderment they experience in the darkness of their grief. Just listen to their heartbroken confession: "We had hoped he was the one to redeem Israel" (v. 21).

I (Bill) was a hospice chaplain for nine years. I discovered from the stories that my patients and their families shared with me just how powerful hope is in directing our lives.[9] I heard stories of how all hope was destroyed when they heard the doctor say, "There's nothing more we can do." As a chaplain, I found that providing patients and their families something new and measurable to hope for was very important. It may have been a patient's hope to see someone before dying, or a mother's hope to see her son graduate from high school.

The two Emmaus disciples had lost all that they hoped for, and they needed someone to help them redefine hope so that they could move forward into their future. This is what all of us have at one time or another experienced in grief. Our hope had to be redefined. Redefining hope usually takes place when we are able to rethink our loss in a larger perspective.

Grief qualifies as one of the great paradigm shifts that people experience. Grief occurs when we lose something that, or someone who, was greatly valued. Not only had the two walking on the road lost a person whom they highly valued, but also the hope that he had instilled in them.

Their response is representative of the larger community of Jesus' disciples, many of whom were certain that the Messiah would overthrow Roman rule and restore Israel to independence. Though Jesus had forecast his future earlier in Jerusalem, which would include suffering and death, his most immediate followers, including Peter, had been reluctant to hear or accept such prophecy (see Matthew 16:21-23).

Isn't this how grief works? We mourn our loss of a person when death claims his or her life, but we also mourn what that life stood for, the potential we saw in it, its unfinished business, and ultimately our loss of all of that, too. In a family setting, it's the grief of a parent who died young, not getting to see a daughter's wedding, or a son's children, or a grandchild's graduation. In a public setting, it's the grief of that national leader who is gone too soon, not being able to fulfill those public policy dreams and goals. In the case of Jesus' disciples, it was the grief of not only losing their friend and mentor, but all the redemption hopes and dreams they had placed in him when it came to Israel's restoration.

Adding to the travelers' confusion is the uncertainty of these resurrection reports that have started their day (vv. 23-24). All of this has left them walking in a fog of bewilderment from Jerusalem to Emmaus. Their minds must have been so preoccupied by the discussion, the reliving of events, and the explanation of it all to this fellow traveler, that we can imagine them arriving at Emmaus with no real memory of the physical trip they took to get there.

It would be similar to a current-day experience of driving somewhere with a preoccupied mind, only to arrive surprised that you are there so soon. This seven-mile walk was filled with mental and conversational activity, seeking to make sense of resurrection news.

That's how a paradigm shift gets underway. Previously held beliefs and practices are questioned to the point of willingness to reexamine them. Jesus, their as-yet-unknown travel companion, next introduces the curriculum for such re-examination. Luke 24:27 tells us, "beginning with Moses and all the prophets, he interpreted to them the things about himself in all the Scriptures."

It was Messiah 101, a complete and thorough review of the old covenant law and prophets, and what they had in fact taught about the Messiah. But now it was seen through a new lens that included the Messiah's suffering, death, and resurrection. Redemption was beginning to be understood in a new way. The work of the

Messiah, including all the long-held assumptions about that work, was now reinterpreted in light of the very ministry activity of Jesus himself, by Jesus himself.

Things were warming up. Minds shifted and sorted. Beliefs were reshaped and formed. Faith was stirred. A new paradigm was close to adoption. Resurrection would be the means by which God would re-order life and redeem people. Soon, over a meal and the breaking of bread, the Emmaus road travelers' eyes were opened, and their hearts burned with the discovery and knowledge that they were the guests of the risen Lord Jesus (vv. 31-32).

Relating to the Story

Have you ever wondered why Jesus' resurrection news was shared in the ways we see it shared in the Gospels? For the most part, these were small and intimate discoveries. Jesus appeared to two travelers on the road and over a meal. He appeared to Mary in the garden. He appeared to small gatherings of his disciples in the upper room and at the beach. There were no large-scale stadium appearances or rallies. By the time of his ascension, several persons had first-hand experiences of the risen Jesus, but they had come little by little, case by case, interpersonally and relationally.

This is not too different than how Jesus shared his entire ministry. He worked through twelve pretty ordinary men, pouring his time and efforts into them, and entrusting to them his ministry legacy. He changed one life at a time with healing miracles and teaching encounters at village wells and tax-collector tables.

This continues today. Whether or not to orient one's life around the resurrection paradigm shift remains a personal choice of faith. It is explained or proclaimed to us person to person, received and examined interpersonally, and ultimately accepted or rejected in that same fashion. But over and over again, when accepted and believed, this paradigm shift has proven to be a difference maker—*the* difference maker—in the lives of multitudes. Since that first

Easter and onward, it has given persons a new understanding of redemption. It has allowed those who have been, or will be, stricken by grief and loss, to yet find hope. It has fueled the movement we know and call the church that has proclaimed to powers and principalities—from Rome's day to this present day—that there is another who is Lord. There is one who is risen and reigns, and we find not only our hope in him, but also our life, abundant now and eternal to come.

Reflection Questions

How has the resurrection changed your life? How might it yet change your viewpoint on the things you've come to know as struggle or hardship? How might it reorient your group, your family, your church to see with eyes that are opened? Where do you need to allow resurrection to speak into your life and leadership?

Questions for Group Discussion or Individual Reflection

1. With which statement, idea, or example about change mentioned in this chapter did you most resonate? Why?
2. When have you felt like quitting as you worked through or with change?
3. As you consider Nieuwhof's five ways to avoid quitting, which one or two have you utilized? Is there one that's new to you? How might you consider using it?
4. Having considered Luke's resurrection narrative, what do you find most surprising about the story and the way it unfolds? With which character(s) do you most identify? Why?
5. Consider the risen Jesus' role in leading his disciples into the paradigm shift of resurrection. What do we learn from his leadership example?
6. What loss have you grieved over that enabled you to identify with the two Emmaus disciples? As a result of your loss, what paradigm shift took place that resurrected your hope?

7. How does the resurrection bring hope to the "change challenges" you face in life—those you confront in your context?

Notes

1. The resurrection is a central event in the Christian faith. We contend that it represents both continuous and discontinuous change. As Fleming Rutledge notes in the quote to follow, it comes as the continuation of God's covenant work with all of creation, but it does so in a way that is discontinuous with prior experience. "In Jesus Christ, and particularly in his cross and resurrection, do we see something entirely new? . . . Does the new dispensation in Jesus of Nazareth follow in a direct line from the Sinai covenant, or is there some sort of break between the two? Is something completely new introduced with the gospel of Christ? This hotly debated question has significant ramifications for New Testament theology. Certainly there is fundamental continuity with the Old Testament in the form of the unconditional covenant made with the patriarch Abraham (Romans 4:1-24; also, Acts 3:25; Galatians 3:14; Hebrews 6:13-15), but there is discontinuity as well (in Luke 3:8 and John 8:56, the references to Abraham are more subversive). Fleming Rutledge, *The Crucifixion: Understanding the Death of Jesus Christ* (Grand Rapids, MI: Eerdmans, 2015), 359.

2. N.T. Wright suggests that Jewish belief in the resurrection grew out of what he calls Second Temple Judaism and was embraced by the Pharisees, a lower class of religious leaders, who saw it as part of a revolutionary worldview that would restore Judaism from its diminished exilic and post-exilic status. This same teaching was a threat to the power of the Sadducees. Here's Wright's commentary: "Resurrection was a revolutionary doctrine, having to do with fiercely held beliefs about the coming climax of Israel's history. It was just the sort of thing, from the Sadducaean point of view, that those troublesome lower-class Pharisees *would* embrace to sustain their revolutionary dreams about the overthrow of the existing order and the establishment of the kingdom of God. The Sadducees' main aim was not to ensure their own personal survival into a future life, but to deny a doctrine that seemed to them (quite rightly) to pose a threat to the survival of their power within the present order and within any coming changes therein." See http://ntwrightpage.com/2016/07/12/christian-origins-and-the-resurrection-of-jesus-the-resurrection-of-jesus-as-a-historical-problem/, accessed December 11, 2018.

3. Jesus also raised the son of the widow of Nain from the dead (Luke 7:11-15) and the daughter of Jairus (Luke 8:41ff).

4. See 1 Kings 17:17-22 for the story of Elijah raising the Zarephath widow's son; 2 Kings 4:32-35, where Elisha raises the son of a Shunammite woman from the dead; and 2 Kings 13:20-21 for the account of a man who was raised from death when his body touched the bones of Elisha.

5. William H. Griffith, *Tears in a Bottle: Learning How to Grieve Well* (Maitland, FL: Xulon Press, 2010), 133.

6. Carey Nieuwhof, *Leading Change without Losing It* (Cumming, GA: The reThink Group, 2012), 107-111.

7. George Bullard suggests that congregations have life cycles that range from birth to death. His belief is that the further along the life cycle a church is toward decline and "old age," the more drastic and disruptive a change in ministry operations is required to give that congregation the hope of re-cycling back to a place of vision and growth. In maturity, empty nest, and retirement, inward-focused behaviors such as placing a priority on relationships, internally focused programming, and maintenance usurp the work of vision. This limits the ability to focus outwardly on programming and relationships characteristic of a church in the process of revitalization. George Bullard, *A Congregational Resource Guide Learning Pathway: "Spiritual Strategic Journey: Tutorial for Congregational Redevelopment"* (Washington, DC: The Alban Institute, 2004), 143.

8. In our book, *8 Questions Jesus Asked,* we discuss Jesus' use of questions as a leadership strategy for inviting persons to participate in their own faith and leadership development. See both the Introduction and Appendix C. Daniel M. Cash and William H. Griffith, *8 Questions Jesus Asked: Discipleship for Leaders* (Valley Forge, PA: Judson Press, 2017), 4–5, 105–106.

9. William H. Griffith, *More Than a Parting Prayer: Lessons in Care-giving for the Dying* (Valley Forge, PA: Judson Press, 2004).

CHAPTER SEVEN

Pentecost

Acts 2:1-42

Change begins when something triggers the individual or group to reflect on their current situation and think about a future they would prefer.[1]

Scripture Encounter

1When the day of Pentecost had come, they were all together in one place. 2And
suddenly from heaven there came a sound like the rush of a violent wind, and it
filled the entire house where they were sitting. 3Divided tongues, as of fire,
appeared among them, and a tongue rested on each of them. 4All of them were
filled with the Holy Spirit and began to speak in other languages, as the Spirit gave
them ability.

5Now there were devout Jews from every nation under heaven living in
Jerusalem. 6And at this sound the crowd gathered and was bewildered, because
each one heard them speaking in the native language of each. 7Amazed and aston-
ished, they asked, "Are not all these who are speaking Galileans? 8And how is it
that we hear, each of us, in our own native language? 9Parthians, Medes, Elamites,
and residents of Mesopotamia, Judea and Cappadocia, Pontus and Asia, 10Phrygia
and Pamphylia, Egypt and the parts of Libya belonging to Cyrene, and visitors
from Rome, both Jews and proselytes, 11Cretans and Arabs—in our own languages
we hear them speaking about God's deeds of power." 12All were amazed and per-
plexed, saying to one another, "What does this mean?" (Acts 2:1-12).

Triggers of Change

"Change begins when something triggers the individual or group to reflect on their current situation and think about a future they would prefer."[2] This quote, from authors Steve Corbett and Brian Fikkert, suggests that the inception of change is related to a triggering event. In their book, *When Helping Hurts*, Corbett and Fikkert write about the challenge of helping persons overcome poverty. Poverty, which can be understood as the insufficiency of income, relationships, physical health, and spiritual fulfillment (and any combination of these factors) is a condition in which many live in perpetuity. It generally takes a trigger to prompt a person toward action and the movement required to change a situation and break out of the cycle of poverty. This trigger provides an image of the future that is more hopeful and positive than the present reality.

These authors suggest that common triggers that initiate change may include a) a recent crisis, b) the burden of the status quo (or present situation) becoming overwhelming, or c) an introduction to a new way of doing or seeing things.[3] As you think back over the paradigm shifts studied in this book, notice how some of the above triggers were present in the change. For example, when Nicodemus went to speak with Jesus in the dark of night, he was responding to a new way of seeing things that Jesus had introduced to him (see chapter three). This new way and new teaching became a trigger in Nicodemus's life that caused him to initiate contact with Jesus and, in time, change his way of thinking and living.

In similar fashion, we suggest that Jesus' kingdom manifesto in which he challenged the status quo of the law by repeatedly saying, "You have heard that it was said [or written], but I tell you," was for some of his audience a trigger for change (see chapter four). It gave them permission to imagine a new or different kind of kingdom than that which their religious experience and tradition had taught.

Even the crisis of Jesus' death by crucifixion and the alarming discovery of his empty tomb triggered in the women and the disciples the possibility of a new understanding of recent events (see chapter six). It created openness in them to reflect on how their experiences lined up with the prior teachings of Jesus. In each of these situations we can find a trigger, and possibly more than one, that caused the change process to begin.

Reflection Questions

Can you identify triggers to change you have experienced that align with these categories: crisis, a new way of seeing or thinking, or the overwhelming nature of the status quo? How often have you attributed that triggering work to the Holy Spirit? Do you believe that God, through the Spirit, is often active in our lives as the trigger for change? We do.

The Scripture in Context

As we reflect on the story of Pentecost in Acts 2, it is possible to make the case that all three of the aforementioned triggers for change were present. We encounter a group of people, followers of Jesus, for whom the religious and political status quo of life has become a burden. Recently, they have experienced a crisis in Jesus' death and resurrection, and they continue to reflect on the new ways of seeing and doing what he taught them. They are primed for change and ready to embrace a new chapter and way of ministry and life that will provide energy, hope, and fulfillment. Pentecost becomes the trigger for their launch into this new chapter.

The event of Pentecost initiates a change of paradigmatic proportion, but, as has been the case in many of the other changes we've studied, Pentecost is change built on a new understanding of a prior experience or faith practice, the Old Testament "Feast of Weeks" (another name for Pentecost). Provisions for this feast can be found in Leviticus 23:15-22, where we read that it was a thanksgiving festival celebrating the last harvest and acknowledging God's abundant provision. It was observed seven weeks and one day (50 days) after the offering of first fruits from the harvest, and it served as a culminating celebration of how God had provided throughout the growing season. The festival also was designed to help the people remember their deliverance from bondage and entrance into the promised land (Leviticus 23:10-11).

The fifty days ("Penta" means fifty) of Pentecost were counted from the Passover festival and first ingathering of the barley crop. Seven weeks, plus one day for the Jubilee, set the date for the Feast of Weeks. It was one of three major festivals in which all Jewish males were expected to make a pilgrimage to, and be present at, the Temple in Jerusalem.[4]

This was the context for the events described in Acts 2. Jesus' disciples had been with him for forty days after his resurrection, and they waited another ten days in Jerusalem, per his instructions for the promise of the Holy Spirit (Acts 1:3-4). They were still there "when the day of Pentecost had come" (Acts 2:1). They were practicing Jews, observing the tradition and festival of their faith, when God, once again, gave new meaning and definition to a faith practice (Pentecost). For the Church, Pentecost would now be forever associated with the coming of the Holy Spirit, fifty days after Easter.

Let's explore the change that this event triggered in the disciples, moving as it did from an observance of their Jewish faith to a defining moment in their Christ-following ministry. Often, Pentecost is called the birthday of the church. But what did this event birth? If we look at Acts 1:6, it appears the disciples are still stuck, even after Jesus' resurrection, in an old paradigm. They asked him, "Lord, is this the time when you will restore the kingdom to Israel?" They are still looking for that earthly revolution when the now-risen Jesus will become king of the nation. Even though they had been present for his teachings about the kingdom, and had heard his kingdom manifesto, they had not completely understood what he was speaking about. Now they anticipate that he will be the *one* to make it all happen, even though Jesus so often has emphasized the role that *they* will play. Now Pentecost, through the coming and filling of the Holy Spirit, empowers the disciples to be fully "on mission" with Christ through the church. It signals a paradigm shift and becomes a major trigger of change. From the day of Pentecost onward, the church begins to grow exponentially and spread geographically. The disciples of Jesus, previously stuck in indecision and past tradition, are suddenly transformed and gifted with unusual and unexplainable abilities (Acts 2:7-12). The event of Pentecost, centered around the coming of the Holy Spirit, triggers that change. Pentecost is so significant in the Christian faith tradition that we speak of it in before and after terms: before and after Pentecost (the coming of the Holy Spirit, the birth of the church).

Relating to the Story

Do you have anything in your life or ministry that is a "before and after" qualifier? In 2008, a major flash flood hit our community, displacing persons from many homes and businesses. The flood is still a "before and after" event in Columbus, Indiana. A trigger for change in our congregation, the flood sparked a mission of service response among us. Nearly every day for two weeks and on a continuing basis for weeks and months afterward, volunteers from our church responded to community needs by forming work parties that helped clean out and repair homes damaged by the flood. Even today, ten years later, church leaders will remark how the flood triggered us to change, causing us to think more about mission and ministry beyond our walls and in the community alongside others. Has a crisis ever triggered change in your congregation?

Pentecost was not a crisis in the life of the disciples, but it was a sudden event that triggered their engagement with others. Speaking in the known languages of the day to a diverse population that had made a pilgrimage to Jerusalem for the Feast of Weeks, the disciples went from being a community cowering behind locked doors to active public evangelists, proclaiming the good news of Christ. In response to the gospel that they preached, persons were called to repentance, baptism, and new life in Christ (Acts 2:38). Three thousand were added to the church on the day of Pentecost, and "day by day the Lord added to their number those who were being saved" (Acts 2:41, 47b). Change—discontinuous with prior experience—had come, triggered by the Holy Spirit.

But let's back up in this story a bit. In Acts 1:4, as Jesus' post-resurrection and pre-ascension time on earth with the disciples draws to a close, he instructs them to "wait" and not leave Jerusalem, promising the coming of the Spirit. So they waited (v. 5). But if you read the remainder of Acts 1, the writer, Luke, in addition to giving us a report of Jesus' ascension, also shares that the apostles take it upon themselves to fill Judas's seat among them. They had been twelve in number prior to Judas's death and wanted to return to twelve in number. Given the history of the twelve tribes of Israel, and longing for the restoration of the kingdom, there was an affinity for the number twelve.

Through a process of casting lots, Matthias, one of two candidates for Judas's seat, is chosen; he was eligible because he met the requirement of having been with Jesus from the beginning of Jesus' baptism until his ascension (Acts 1:21-22). After he is chosen by the eleven, we never hear about Matthias again; he does not appear in the rest of the Scripture story. We find this interesting. We also note that it is not recorded in Scripture that Jesus asked the eleven to replace Judas. Could it be that they are, in their anxiousness, determined to take this action on their own, without God's direction? Might Paul, and not Matthias, have been God's choice for Judas's seat? We cannot be sure, so we only speculate, but there are experiences in our own journeys of faith that have helped us learn the importance of waiting on the Spirit and not getting ahead of God with our plans.

I (Bill) remember when I was ready to move out of youth ministry and accept the position of pastoring a church. That longing came during a period of months that I was invited to fill the pulpit of the American Baptist church in the town where I lived, which was ten miles from the church where I served. The pastor of that church was terminally ill, so another associate and I would take turns filling the pulpit. I quickly realized that pastoral ministry was what I was called to do.

I worked through the denomination's personnel connections, and my name was sent to a number of churches, each of which responded the same way: "We are looking for someone with pastoral experience." I was discouraged.

One evening I was home with our son while my wife, Lois, was at work, and the doorbell rang. When I opened the door, there stood three men from the church in my community where I had been filling the pulpit. By this time the pastor had died, and I had been called upon to fill other pastoral needs, so I assumed a need had arisen about which they needed to talk with me.

When we were all seated, one of the men said, "We are here to invite you to become our pastor." I was speechless. The man continued, "The church has met and sees no need to have a formal time when you come and candidate since you have been filling in as our pastor over these last months."

I was still momentarily at a loss for an appropriate response. My first thought was a quick "Yes!" However, there was an issue that was being addressed by both the church I was serving and this church. The church I was serving had been studying the possibility of beginning a single ministry or church in two locations: the inner city and the suburbs. We had spent months visiting other churches and had just come to the decision to offer the church where I had been filling in the option of uniting with us to create the new dual-location ministry. I knew the timeline for a final decision was to be made the following week. I also knew if the church accepted the offer, I was not interested in being on the multiple staff that would provide leadership. I wanted my own pastoral ministry.

My response to the offer to become pastor was to buy some time, so I asked my three visitors for time to pray about their offer. They understood completely. I needed to do more than buy some time, however. I needed to discern just what God's will was for my future ministry. I could have said yes at that moment because I felt excited about the offer, but until a definitive decision was made on the possible joint effort, I needed to wait. I told the men what day I would call and give them my response.

The day after the decision was made at the church that I was serving, my senior pastor announced in our staff meeting that the other church had refused the offer to merge. My heart was pounding because I knew I was going to make a call that evening and accept the offer to be their pastor. As anxious as I was to accept when the offer was made, I knew waiting was necessary to be sure and know the Spirit's leading. And now fifty years later, I am so thankful I waited.

Perhaps you also know what it is to wait. The importance of Jesus' command to wait can apply when we feel the burden of the status quo as a trigger for change. Have you noticed that the church often tolerates the status quo more than other societal institutions do? Perhaps it is our need to be and act nice that causes us to put up with ineffective and outdated approaches much longer than is healthy. We are afraid of offending someone. We don't want to hurt a long-standing member's feelings or rock the boat and cause people we love to lose their footing, so we put up with things that for-profit organizations would not tolerate. For example, we don't replace the ineffective volunteer, or we neglect to clear the church rolls of inactive members. We may allow a long-tenured staff member to coast to retirement, or a long-ago diminished ministry to continue and divert funds from other needs. It's pretty hard to buck the status quo. How many times have we seen a new leader (professional or volunteer) try to effect immediate change in a status-quo situation only to be rebuffed as the system (made up, of course, of people) resists that change? This frustrates new leaders and sometimes causes them to resign. Perhaps there is some rationale for a waiting period, as was the case for the disciples, before wholesale change is adopted. This was the case for Bill as he was patient in allowing circumstances to evolve.

If waiting is not just passivity, but time spent learning and in discernment, it often can bear good fruit when change is eventually pursued. Waiting, in a spirit of discernment, can allow a leader to assess the situation, including the challenges that will need to be addressed as change is introduced. Waiting, bathed in prayer, can help a leader become informed about the organization's history, prior attempts at change, victories and defeats, and the available resources from which to fuel the work of change.

What does the Scripture say Jesus' disciples did during those ten days of waiting between his ascension and the Holy Spirit's descent? In addition to electing Matthias as Judas's replacement, they "were constantly devoting themselves to prayer" (Acts 1:14). This season of prayer rooted them spiritually to be in a position to receive what was about to come. Their wait is not to be dismissed as insignificant. Such prayerful waiting, before the Lord, can awaken passion and expectation in a group, creating readiness among those who may previously have grown content or complacent or allowed fear to overtake them.

This leads us to reflect on the third trigger for change identified above: the introduction of a new way of doing and seeing things. Both Jesus in his ministry with the disciples, and the Holy Spirit in inspiring their Pentecost-prompted acts, introduced new ways of seeing and doing. Pentecost marks the launch of the church's mission. The Book of Acts, often called the Acts of the Apostles, might be more appropriately named the Acts of the Holy Spirit, for it is the Spirit who inspires and motivates these Christ followers to travel to far and distant places proclaiming the gospel and calling persons into response to God's saving acts. The Spirit instills a confidence and vision in Peter and the others that moves the mission ever forward. No longer is this a backward-looking group. Now, with the Spirit's help, they are imagining a future much more in tune with Jesus' kingdom message. They are becoming the message.

A leader's role in the imagining of a new future is critical in the work of change. Like the Hebrew people before us, our churches are filled with people who want to go back—back to Egypt, back to the glory days of the church (whatever they may be remembered as being), but there is no going back when it comes to leading change today. On a couple of occasions, I (Dan) have acquiesced to congregational voices that wanted to revisit some past experience that was monumental in the church's story. One time, we revisited a lay-driven spiritual renewal weekend that had been terrifically successful about twenty years before in the life of this particular congregation. The ministry involved a traveling team of lay leaders, plucked and trained from various congregations across the region, who came to lead a renewal weekend in the local context. I had heard about this past experience multiple times and, wanting to encourage ownership of ministry, I agreed that we should pursue it once again.

We contacted the regional leadership team members, followed their advice and steps right down to the last detail, and welcomed them into our community for the weekend. Afterwards, we wondered why the experience, while good, did not live up to the past memory. We discovered that you cannot go back. We discovered that either the memory of this past event had grown into a legendary spiritual experience of unreachable proportion, or we just lived in a very different day when life happens at a different pace, with different needs, technologies, and circumstances. In other words, the weekend failed to connect as it had years before. As one person told me, the only thing good about the good old days is that they are over!

A leader has to learn to resist the cries for a return to yesteryear, however great it may have been. The leader's role, when it comes to preparing a church for change, is to help the church imagine the future. The good news is that we have terrific resources and partners in this work. Let's start with the Spirit. The Spirit is that member of the Trinity who nudges, prompts, and pulls people forward. As we pray—together and individually—for change in the congregation, the Spirit is at work in our hearts. A leader's role is to remind people of this, and to invite them to become open, as well as to share what the Spirit is saying.

Jesus' ministry, as recorded in the Gospels, is another terrific resource for the leader who wants to prepare people for change. Do we ever see Jesus saying, "I don't think we can do this, People!" Or, "This is just going to be too hard." Or, "We tried that once, remember?" No! Jesus is always calling people to "come" so they can then "go." Come to me. Come and follow. Come together. Then, go and serve. Go and preach. Go and proclaim. Go and heal. Go and lead. Jesus works in partnership with the Spirit. In John 20:21, Jesus, appearing to his disciples after his resurrection, says: "As the Father has sent me, so I send you." Do you remember what happens next? "[H]e breathed on them and said to them, 'Receive the Holy Spirit'" (20:22).

In this great paradigm shift, the disciples are now empowered to carry forward Jesus' ministry. They also have a partner in the Holy Spirit. Good leaders will remind those whom they lead of this promise. Good leaders use all the tools available to them to stoke the imagination of God's people. These tools include preaching, Bible study, prayer, one-on-one conversations, and personal testimony; group, team, and committee work; blogs; and social, digital, and print media. Good leaders are the cheerleaders, coaches, counselors, consultants, co-workers, collaborators, prophets, proclaimers, and imaginers of change. If the leader does not believe in the change, why would anyone else? Good leaders help us imagine a future that is bright, hopeful, and possible.

Returning to the Scripture in Context

In Acts 2, Peter, empowered by the Spirit, provides a model of good leadership. He becomes the spokesman to defend and explain what is happening. His words and actions demonstrate an understanding of the Spirit that has come upon him. The Spirit has led him to assume a new boldness in preaching a sermon on the saving works of Christ. The Spirit has given him permission to leave behind the old paradigm of faith and proclaim something new to the crowd that is gathered for the Feast of Weeks. Peter is an early adopter of the change he now calls others to embrace.

His first action is to confront the scoffers. The initial response of the crowd to the changed disciples, speaking in different languages through the power of the Spirit, is to assume they are drunk (Acts 2:13). Peter does not allow that storyline to gain traction, stating, "These are not drunk, as you suppose, for it is only nine o'clock in the morning" (2:15). But he doesn't stop there. In addition to confronting those who are skeptical of what they see and hear, Peter helps interpret what they see. He roots the experience in Scripture, quoting a passage from Joel 2:28 and following. He moves on, in his Pentecost sermon, to link the manifestation of the Spirit they are witnessing to the life, death, and resurrection of Jesus, and to call his audience in response to the gospel to "repent and be baptized" (2:38).

Peter's actions give us an example for those who would lead change; namely, that the change leader must be prepared to refute those who scoff and express skepticism. Experience tells us that such negative reactions are common responses to change. Therefore, we should not be surprised by them because people often are mystified by the results that come from the Spirit and acts of the Spirit, as expressed in the words, actions, and outcomes of empowered leaders and believers. Miraculous healings, charismatic expressions of prayer and worship, and bold actions in the name of ministry can be puzzling to those unfamiliar with such things, just as they were to Peter's audience. Notice how he responds. Peter simply offers a different understanding than the one the skeptics have proposed. He roots his explanation in Scripture, all of which serves to reorient the experience and keep it from being derailed. This shows us that confronting skepticism does not need to be argumentative, which serves only to ratchet up the opposition; instead, it can be direct.

If we, as leaders, can root the changes or reasons for the changes we propose in Scripture, it will help the faith community to see them as more than the latest theory or program. Peter gives us a good example of a faith leader employing the language and understandings of faith to help his audience come to grips with the change they experience. In doing so, he helps move the interpretation of that day's events from a human cause and effect to actions clearly attributable to God.

A Spiritual Word of Caution

Before we leave this text and topic of the Spirit, as it relates to leading change, we would like to acknowledge that often Spirit talk can carry a certain amount of baggage. As the following examples demonstrate, much damage has been done in the name of the Holy Spirit when that sacred name has been used as a hammer to put down those judged to be less spiritual, or as a wedge to separate and divide traditions and groups with different theological understandings, or as an excuse to manipulate persons through the use of spiritual language and innuendo. Too often, such misuse of the Spirit happens in the name of change. How can we guard against it?

One way we guard against falling into these traps is to continuously watch our attitude when it comes to all things spiritual. Having an understanding that one is Spirit-filled, or pursuing change and direction by being Spirit-led, does not mean we are better than others. Some of the most spirit-filled persons we have known are those who live very humble lives. These persons do not call attention to themselves through demonstrative acts or loud talk. Rather, they are reflective and unassuming souls in our midst who obediently follow the Spirit's guidance in behind-the-scenes servant leadership roles. They walk with the Spirit daily and depend on the Spirit in all that they do. You probably know someone like this.

In correcting the crowd through his preaching, Peter did not assume an attitude of superiority. He laid out the truth clearly and invited persons to respond to it. He also did not claim the spotlight all for himself. Others were prophesying that day, too, and sharing God's message. Substantive paradigm-shifting change requires such collaboration. There is room for more than one voice; indeed, there is room for an entire orchestra of voices being directed by the Holy Spirit.

A related warning along these lines concerns the use of language or what we might call "spirit talk." This can be one of the hardest parts of discernment: feeling you have a message or directive from the Lord but not being arrogant about it. Those who speak and lead change under the guidance of the Spirit carry a burden to be judicious and careful in knowing the Spirit's leading before speaking words such as, "The Spirit told me." In fact, we would suggest avoiding a phrase like that, or its companion phrase, "God spoke to me."

It is hard for others to argue with that kind of statement, because to do so is to have our response framed as though we are arguing against God. If one speaks boldly with such words as "the Spirit revealed this to me," and another who has been praying about the same query feels that she has received insight that is diametrically opposed to that message, which one has the Spirit's leading? Perhaps neither one, or perhaps it is time for them to bring those opposite viewpoints into dialogue with one another in the continuing work of finding the mind of Christ.

Spirit talk is like a congregant suggesting that all will be well in a church's ministry if "we just get back to preaching the Word." There is a distinct judgment that accompanies that sentence, whether it is intended or not. The judgment suggests that "we" have not been preaching the Word. Yet, for the diligent and devoted preacher or Bible study leader who spends hours each week with the Word in preparation for the preaching or teaching moment, such a flippant and cliché phrase can be offensive. He or she knows the Word is being preached and taught—perhaps just not in the manner the critic is looking to hear it. The point we are making is to choose your words carefully and think about what you are saying. "Think before speaking" is a good rule of thumb!

Finally, when it comes to leading by the Spirit, the apostle Paul gives us perhaps the best metric by which to measure such leadership. In Galatians 5:22-23, he lists what he calls the fruit of the Spirit: love, joy, peace, patience, kindness, generosity, faithfulness, gentleness, and self-control. The presence in our lives of these qualities of the fruit of the Spirit is indicative of a life lived in step with the Holy Spirit. An over-emphasis on the gifts and power of the Spirit, without equal time being given to our need to bear spiritual fruit, is an abuse of the Spirit's role. When leading change, our exemplifying the qualities inherent in the fruit of the Spirit will come in handy and help persons believe that we care about them.

All of the above should be considered within the call to embrace and live into the Spirit paradigm shift of Acts 2!

The day of Pentecost and descent of the Holy Spirit changed everything for the early followers of Jesus. It ushered them into a completely new paradigm for community, which became known as the church. This same Holy Spirit continues to call persons today into the exciting work of change. One never quite knows what will trigger such a journey. Will it be a crisis that is embraced as an opportunity, the burden of the status quo that can no longer be tolerated and gives way to a collaborative process of imagination, or a new way of seeing and doing things voiced by a leader whom persons would be eager to both follow and partner with? Trigger points come in congregations. Attentive leaders recognize and respond to them, helping us not to miss them when they happen.

Questions for Group Discussion or Individual Reflection

1. What have you experienced as a trigger that led to change? What happened?
2. How have you experienced the Holy Spirit as an initiator or companion to change? What do you think is the Spirit's primary role?
3. How does your congregation acknowledge or celebrate Pentecost?
4. What part of the Pentecost story do you find yourself wanting to learn more about?
5. Which trigger for change is most evident in your congregation (or personal situation) today: a) a crisis, b) the burden of the status quo, or c) a new way of thinking and seeing? How are you responding to that trigger?

Notes

1. Steve Corbett and Brian Fikkert, *When Helping Hurts: How to Alleviate Poverty without Hurting the Poor . . . and Yourself.* (Chicago: Moody Publishers, 2012), 207–208.
2. Corbett and Fikkert, 207–208.
3. Corbett and Fikkert, 208.
4. The other two Jewish pilgrimage festivals were the Feast of Unleavened Bread (Passover) and the Feast of Booths (Sukkoth).

CHAPTER EIGHT

Everybody Welcome!

Acts 10:34-48; 13:23-52; 15:1-35

Change takes time. The deep transformational movement from the come-to orientation of churches shaped in the 20th century to the go-to church so crucial in the 21st century will take time as well.[1]

Scripture Encounter

[34]Then Peter began to speak to them: "I truly understand that God shows no partiality, [35]but in every nation anyone who fears him and does what is right is acceptable to him. [36]You know the message he sent to the people of Israel, preaching peace by Jesus Christ—he is Lord of all. [37]That message spread throughout Judea, beginning in Galilee after the baptism that John announced: [38]how God anointed Jesus of Nazareth with the Holy Spirit and with power; how he went about doing good and healing all who were oppressed by the devil, for God was with him. [39]We are witnesses to all that he did both in Judea and in Jerusalem. They put him to death by hanging him on a tree; [40]but God raised him on the third day and allowed him to appear, [41]not to all the people but to us who were chosen by God as witnesses, and who ate and drank with him after he rose from the dead. [42]He commanded us to preach to the people and to testify that he is the one ordained by God as judge of the living and the dead. [43]All the prophets testify about him that everyone who believes in him receives forgiveness of sins through his name."

[44]While Peter was still speaking, the Holy Spirit fell upon all who heard the word. [45]The circumcised believers who had come with Peter were astounded that the gift of the Holy Spirit had been poured out even on the Gentiles, [46]for they heard them speaking in tongues and extolling God. Then Peter said, [47]"Can anyone withhold the water for baptizing these people who have received the Holy Spirit just as we have?" [48]So he ordered them to be baptized in the name of Jesus Christ. Then they invited him to stay for several days (Acts 10:34-48).

Relating to the Story

Change takes time. Complex, adaptive change in long-established congregations takes time. Wise leaders will come to understand this as they work among those congregations, pursuing a pace of change that is both palatable and effective. In this chapter, we will explore a final scriptural paradigm shift that we believe illustrates this truth. This shift happened over time in the life of the early church during the leadership of persons like Peter and Paul. The Holy Spirit, through the apostles' steady and persistent leadership, brought about a new movement—the church—in which everyone was welcome, but it did not happen overnight.

Scot McKnight uses the metaphor of a salad to describe the diverse makeup of the early church. He suggests that a good and interesting salad has a lot of variety. It is a mix of different vegetables, nuts, and fruit which make it much more interesting than a generic wedge of iceberg lettuce with a few croutons thrown on top.[2] But the formation of such a salad takes some time and effort. Mixing all those ingredients together requires prep time with each one of them. A good and seasoned cook will understand that you don't create such a masterpiece in an instant. It takes some time.

McKnight says the early church was a "fellowship of differents"—a salad with great variety—which made it so interesting. The church combined persons from diverse backgrounds and social norms. As it is described in Acts and elsewhere in the New Testament, the church was a mix of "differents": Jews and Gentiles, slaves and free, men and women, wealthy and poor. Within these differing categories one can assume even more diversity in vocation, education, living arrangements, personality, and interests. It truly was a fellowship of differents. The church represented a major change for those who came to be mixed together in this new salad bowl.

Many of the paradigm shifts of faith that we have examined in this book are in some way related to the Old Testament Law and what persons had long come to accept as God's expectation and guidance for their lives. The prophets, Jesus, Peter, and Paul (among others) called for a shift in understanding many facets of these long-held beliefs by introducing change that we've identified in prior chapters, including the incarnation, being "born again," a new understanding of the kingdom of God, a new covenant, resurrection, and Pentecost. Each of these shifts was the equivalent of the effect of putting new wine in an old wineskin or sewing a new piece of cloth to patch an old garment. This was change that rocked the foundation by seismic shift-shattering of former sacred traditions. At the very least, the change caused persons to re-examine what they believed.

The change was introduced over a lengthy period of time in order to prepare for, and bring about, the formation of the church. Such paradigmatic shifts helped establish the Christian faith by assuring that the followers of Jesus did not just become a sect within Judaism, but a world-wide movement where everyone would be welcome. It would take years of preaching, teaching, and debate for this shift to occur. In fact, one might argue that our ability to completely embrace the fellowship of differents that Christ has called forth in the church has been hindered by our inability to fully emerge from the lengthy process of having our old beliefs challenged.

Transformational change that we have studied in this book requires what Eugene Peterson often calls "a long obedience in the same direction."[3] That is to say it does not happen quickly. As the early church and her leaders grappled with the inclusion of those whom they were previously taught to be outsiders (Gentiles, women, slaves), they had to confront old beliefs again and again. In similar fashion, congregational leaders working to effect transformational change today are required to take this long and faithful approach. The image that sometimes has been applied to the work of transformational change within a congregation is that of turning around an ocean liner. It takes a long time and a lot of space to do this. By one estimation, while you can make a U-turn in a row boat in about eight feet, to do so in an ocean liner requires fourteen miles![4] In addition to the time and space required, a strong, steady, and determined hand must be at the wheel if such a change in direction is going to be accomplished.

The Scripture in Context

Peter and Paul, both apostles and leaders in the early church, were central to helping bring about the changes of inclusion that we have identified above. Primarily, Peter was called to minister and lead among his Jewish brothers and sisters while Paul was called as an apostle to evangelize among the Gentiles. Both had difficult assignments requiring that "long obedience" spoken of previously.

In Acts 10, Peter has a vision, making plain to him that "God shows no partiality" but "in every nation [accepts] anyone who fears him and does what is right" (v. 34). He initially struggles with this vision and new message, which we see early in the Acts 10 narrative, where Peter says, "I have never eaten anything that is profane or unclean" (v. 14). Luke, the author of the Book of Acts, comments, "Peter was greatly puzzled . . ." (v. 17). This seems to be clear evidence that Peter's old paradigm of thought is firmly rooted.

Yet a new paradigm is also emerging. Consider this verse, describing Peter's encounter with Cornelius: "You yourselves know that it is unlawful for a Jew to associate with or to visit a Gentile; but God has shown me that I should not call anyone profane or unclean" (v. 28). It is this new understanding and insight that led Peter to go with the delegation to Cornelius's home in Ceasarea and proclaim his message to a mixed audience of both Jews and Gentiles. While he preached, "the Holy Spirit fell upon *all* who heard the word" (v. 44, emphasis added). This event is sometimes referred to as the Gentile Pentecost, an outpouring of the Holy Spirit that was very similar to what took place in Acts 2.

Peter was the recognized leader of Jesus' disciples, and his voice would hold great credibility for others as they grappled with this shift in practice—the inclusion of Gentiles into the faith community. As we shall see, however, it would take time for this shift to become fully cemented.

Paul knew that his call to the Gentiles would be hard for the Jews to understand, so in his journey from city to city he went to the local synagogue to address the Jews first. This was done to assure them that he was not rejecting them or his Jewish heritage and tradition. Acts 13:13-52 provides an example of Paul's pattern of engagement as it takes place in the city of Antioch. Initially, he was well received in the synagogue and was even invited back to speak the next day. Many of the Gentiles responded favorably to Paul's message (v. 48). "But the Jews incited the devout women of high standing and the leading men of the city, and stirred up persecution against Paul and Barnabas, and drove them out of their region" (v. 50). An old paradigm was threatened by the new; though change was introduced, it would require more time to fully take root.

Relating to the Scripture Story

We stated above that Peter represented a credible voice among his peers as he led them toward change. Over time the same would be true of Paul, who would prove his faithfulness and effectiveness in ministry with the Gentiles as the leaders of the Jerusalem church took note.[5] Identifying those credible voices within a congregation can go a long way toward helping change occur. The voice may belong to a pastoral leader, but it also may be that of a trusted lay leader—perhaps one who has been with the congregation for a good length of time. New pastoral leaders, anxious to effect change, sometimes resent that they are not initially seen as a credible voice, but it takes time to earn trust and respect, as Paul did, and to establish a record of faithfulness. Rather than resent this process, a new pastoral leader would be wise not only to identify the existing credible voices in the congregation, but to work alongside them in introducing and leading change.

Early in ministry, I (Dan) served a congregation that experienced growth and wanted to accommodate that growth through an expansion of the church facility. This was accomplished in a couple of phases: a remodeling of the existing facility, followed a few years later by a sizeable addition. I was twenty-five years old with no real vocational experience when I started serving that church. As the saying goes, I knew enough to be dangerous, but I did know enough to make sure the recognized credible voices of leadership within the congregation were on board with these projects and taking a leading role in their implementation. Because they were on board, however, we were able to make significant changes not only in the facility, but in leadership expansion and growth in a relatively short amount of time (seven years).

In contrast to that experience, let's consider my present place of pastoral leadership. I (Dan) have long felt that part of the reason I was called as pastor at the FBC, Columbus, Indiana, was to help the congregation through change. This has been an interest of mine throughout my ministry, as well as an identified need I have seen in many churches today. We have been able to serve together well and accomplish much in ministry, but I never imagined that we would be ten years into our partnership of ministry as pastor and people before we seriously took up the issues of adaptive change. As I reflect on those ten years, I do not believe that the reason it took that span of time was because we were avoiding change, for much was happening in that decade that prepared the way for change. Part of what happened was my building credibility and trust with the congregation to be a voice of leadership and change they would be willing to work alongside through the challenges this change would present. Remember, when it comes to leading change, we've all got our ocean liner!

The pace at which you are able to address and lead change may be different in one place than in another. Each situation has its own story, its own obstacles and its own timetable. A younger church may be able to change much quicker than a congregation with a 165-year-old history. Also, the demographic makeup of the congregation will determine the pace at which change is acceptable. In general, younger generations have grown up in a world where change is constant. This may make them more pliable than older generations. Also, length of tenure in the congregation will make a difference. A forty-year-old who has known only one congregation may have a harder time with change in his church than a seventy-year-old who has been part of the same congregation for only five years. Many factors are involved in setting the pace. We will return to a few more of these later.

Returning to the Scripture Story

Acts 15:1-35 might be viewed as ground zero for the clash between the old and new paradigms through which Peter and Paul are helping lead the emerging church. This passage recounts the story of the Jerusalem Council, a gathering of recognized early church leaders (apostles and elders) who take up the matter of Gentile inclusion. The debate, in part, concerns whether or not such inclusion requires the full adoption of Jewish practices, including circumcision. It is important to bear in mind that by now years have passed since the initial admittance of Gentiles into the church had begun. Paul and Barnabas, and to some extent Peter, have a track record of ministry with the Gentile populations in the locations where the three have witnessed the Gentiles come to faith in Christ and receive the Holy Spirit. The testimony that Paul, Barnabas, and Peter share before the Jerusalem Council verifies this very point (v. 4). However, there still is resistance to this change, principally from some believers who belong to the sect of the Pharisees and insist on full adoption of the law of Moses by any who would be part of the church (v. 5).

The credible voices that help guide the council in their discernment belong to Peter and Paul (vv. 7-12). Notice, also, that the additional voices of Barnabas and James are named among those who speak (vv. 12-13). It is James who draws the council's attention to the witness of Scripture (vv. 16-17). It would seem that the leadership of the council is determined to listen to both the human voices and the experiences they've had, and especially to the voice of God (through Scripture) in this matter. Did it happen quickly? No. This was a change process that took years to adopt. In this pinnacle meeting, leaders representing differing viewpoints had to agree to a process of debate and discernment. This was hard work, but in the end the Jerusalem Council decided that "we should not trouble those Gentiles who are turning to God, but we should write to them to abstain only from things polluted by idols and from fornication and from whatever has been strangled and from blood" (vv. 19-20). Notice that a change was decided, companioned by a means of communicating and implementing that change.

A letter and delegation were sent forth from the council to share the news (see Acts 15:22-30). In taking these steps, the council broadened the ownership of the change to include "the consent of the whole church" (v. 22). Others who owned the change were a leadership implementation team that consisted of both familiar faces—Paul and Barnabas—and leaders from the Jerusalem church—Judas, called Barabbas, and Silas (v. 22). A new paradigm of faith was beginning to become real. Everyone was welcome.

Relating to the Story

Perhaps, as you read this chapter, you are mindful of a change you and your congregation are facing. You may be in the thick of leading others through that change, or at a beginning point with the change and not sure where to begin. You may be feeling the pressure to "make something happen." You may have inherited a change discussion and challenge that the congregation has been bumping into for years. You may be wondering what a realistic timeline is for implementation of such a change, or how to pace yourself and others through the steps and process of change. You may be puzzled as to how to find the time and energy to work on this change, while keeping all the other existing ministries going. We would encourage you to pay attention to the paradigm shift we explore in this chapter as you think through all of the above scenarios that may ring true to your context. The change adopted in Acts 15—the full inclusion of those from a Gentile background, and the emergence of the church in which all were welcome—evolved over a period of years. One might argue that in the church we still wrestle with this change today.

Determining Your Pace

Many factors may be involved as you determine the pace at which to work toward change in your ministry context. Each faith community will have its own history and participants, as well as unique obstacles to change. We acknowledge this in order to avoid over-simplifying what may be complex situations. Nonetheless, we do feel that often there are some common factors that impact the pace at which complex and adaptive change can be pursued. Among these are 1) the complexity or size of the challenge being faced, 2) the composition of the group being led through change, and 3) the leadership style(s) of those involved. We will use the theme of "everybody's welcome" discussed in this chapter, and some of our own personal experiences, to address these three general factors that impact the pace of change.

Determining the Pace of Change

As we previously stated, many of the changes facing the church today are complex in nature and require an adaptive response. Because the challenges inherent in the change process are so complex, we often find ourselves with little prior experience in meeting them, so doing so calls for a pace that is deliberate. The urgency we feel in needing to make changes can sometimes propel us to quick action that may undercut any real chance we have in shifting the paradigm. A more thoughtful and reflective pace will create space for ownership and participation. We see this in tracking the inclusion of the Gentiles into the early church, a process that took place over several years and moved at a fairly deliberate pace after Pentecost.

While that change was of a grand scale and scope, some of the more frustrating challenges we confront in congregational change today may be very specific and local. We will illustrate this point through a couple of personal ministry experiences.

Let's start with a story about a heating and cooling system (HVAC). Years ago, most church buildings were not equipped with air conditioning. In many parts of the country, including the Midwest, air conditioning was seen as an extravagant addition to one's facility and budget. Persons may not have had this luxury in their homes, so the expense of adding it to a public building where it would not be used several months of the year was prohibitive. But attitudes and lifestyles began to change. New homes were built with HVAC systems, not just heating systems. Also, because public spaces (offices, schools, libraries, restaurants) are now routinely cooled, persons began to expect this convenience in their lives. Now church facilities without air conditioning presented persons with another obstacle and reason to stay home on a hot summer Sunday.

The congregation in which I (Dan) served in the late 1980s and early 1990s was one of those facilities that did not have an air conditioning system. In fact, there had been long-standing arguments as to the merit of adding a system "that would only be used a couple of hours each week."[6] In addition, the physical and structural challenges of retrofitting an existing facility with this modern convenience were real, as were the economic obstacles; but so was the heat, the humidity, and the misery of a hot and stuffy worship space. Often, on a summer Sunday, I would sweat through my clothing as I led worship and preached. In a congregation that was growing younger, where most adults experienced the presence of air conditioning in all other facets of their lives, its absence in the church facility was increasingly problematic.

Therefore, an education campaign began, sharing the importance of this once-felt convenience as an expectation in modern society. Professional HVAC representatives were consulted and able to share presentations on improvements in technology and installation. Persons were given time and space to reflect on all of the above. It did not hurt that we had a particularly hot summer with a couple of church weddings that packed out the house where we watched the wedding party melt before our eyes. One of these weddings, which I will not soon forget, utilized two large heart-shaped candelabras in the rather intimate chancel space—fully lit and greatly elevating the temperature of the room. I felt I was conducting a nuptials ceremony in "a ring of fire" (Johnny Cash's song lyrics running through my head as I led the bridal couple through their vows). At the very next congregational meeting the decision to air condition the facility was made with little objection. Nevertheless, it was a change process that had occurred over time (years) and that was taken at a deliberate pace.

In subsequent ministry partnerships, I have revisited that process as I worked with congregations on other complex changes, including installing modern technology in worship and education space, adding alternative worship options to accommodate differences in style and preference, and addressing issues of culture change around discussions of revitalization. None of this was quick work. It all required a deliberate and steady pace that honored persons' need to understand, reflect, discuss, and determine next steps.

In one of the churches that I served as pastor, I (Bill) had two full-time associate staff colleagues who provided direction for the Education and Youth ministries. After a couple of years, I saw a need for a staff person to provide direction for the Music Ministry. As I approached the church council to share this vision, I sensed that there might be some opposition because the part-time person who led the choir was a church member. The council advised me to sit down with that person and explain my vision and how it would increase the music ministry of the congregation. It was difficult both to affirm the good that had been done by the person, as well as to suggest that the vision would include calling someone who had professional training in directing different types of church choirs. The person was upset with the idea, which I could understand, but I was convinced that the church could make a decision.

Numerous meetings were held; over a period of nine months, everyone had opportunities to share in the process. Finally, after a special meeting was announced and held, discussions were shared and a vote was taken. The hiring of new ministry staff persons was nearly unanimously approved except for a couple of folks who were friends with the choir director. As I look back on the life of that congregation, I see this change in staff as a major shift that has provided great value to them. By the time I retired from the congregation, the newly hired associate had built a music ministry of seven different choirs (voice and handbells), from small children to senior adults. The process and pace of change had been effective. It would have taken much more time for the congregation to own the vision had it simply been handed down from the leader.

Another factor that bears weight in determining the pace at which you are able to pursue change is the composition of the group with whom you work. The more diverse the group, the more important will be your attentiveness to pace. The early church that we read of in Acts is a good example. Let's consider again the diversity of this fellowship of differents. We already have acknowledged diversity in the broad categories of male/female, slave/free, and Jew/Gentile, but these categories do not take into account the differences in personality, life experience, vocational role, and ways of thinking. What might this have looked like in one of the apostle Paul's house churches, composed of about thirty persons? Consider this description by Peter Oakes[7]:

Approximate Make-Up of a Pauline House Church

- A craft worker in whose home they meet, along with his wife, children, a couple of male slaves, a female domestic slave, and a dependent relative

- Some tenants, with families and slaves and dependents, also living in the same home in rented rooms
- Some family members of a householder who himself does not participate in the church
- A couple of slaves whose owners do not attend
- Some freed slaves who do not participate in the church
- A couple of homeless people
- A few migrant workers renting small rooms in the home.

Now compare this with the mental picture you have of your congregation and its diversity of generations, genders, theological viewpoints, life experiences, education levels, employment and vocational roles (professional, blue collar, business, and farm), personal interests, and so forth. The composition of any group needs to be considered as you lead it into and through complex adaptive change. We often underestimate the time and patience that will be required to re-route the ocean liner we know and love. Pace is important.

Leadership style is another factor that impacts the pace of change. When we compare what we know of Peter, Paul, Barnabas, and James we can imagine a few different leadership styles. Peter, at times, appeared to be rather impulsive. Paul was driven. Barnabas may have been more pastoral, wanting to give persons encouragement, whereas the little we know of James shows him in a more reflective light, drawing persons to Scripture. William Barclay suggests that James's "leadership was not that of an official office; it was a moral leadership conceded to him because he was an outstanding man."[8]

Combine the above diverse leadership styles into a team and imagine the meetings! There must have been times of debate as they came to consensus in the Jerusalem Council. We do not see a rush to voting, letting the majority (maybe even simple majority) rule. There was a more measured and deliberate pace that accommodated these different leaders and helped them to arrive together at the Council's decision (Acts 15:28).

Leadership today is conducted through a variety of styles, just as it was in the first-century church. In congregational systems, persons come with leadership models learned in the military (directive, chain of command), the business world (team-based), the world of education (collaborative), and various other backgrounds. Meshing those styles together in a community is part of that fellowship of differents. It can be rather interesting—and frustrating. The executive who is used to making decisions and getting things done may push for a quicker pace. The manager, who is comfortable in the work of organization, may quickly jump to categorize and organize thoughts and outcomes. The counselor, who is at home with exploration of feelings and process, may call for a slower and more reflective pace.

Often, it becomes the pastoral leader's role to call persons to a deliberate pace that honors their faith identity. Engagement in theological reflection (using tools like Scripture, tradition, and experience) requires a different pace and rhythm than corporate or club life. The leader will need to communicate how this process may differ from other models, why it is worth the time, and when group engagement will occur. Also, the leader will need to have a personal comfort level with a process that is not always tidy or neat. By modeling the ability to refrain from being anxious while present in the confusion of change, a leader offers others in the process a gift of his or her example. There will be many loose ends as the change work proceeds, but if one remembers that it is work worth doing, the confusion and chaos of the process can be tolerated, if not enjoyed.

Norms That Can Guide Reflection on Change

In addition to leading change by modeling a non-anxious presence, pastoral and lay leaders alike can help establish the pace of change by inviting the group into a process of theological reflection. Traditionally, there are three dominant norms that guide such a process of reflection: Scripture, tradition, and experience. We might think of these as a three-legged stool.

In the change work in which Peter, Paul, James, and Barnabas engaged in Acts, we find all three norms at work. In Acts 15:16-17, James appears to quote from Amos 9:11-12. In doing so, like Peter before him on the day of Pentecost in Acts 2:17-21 (quoting Joel 2:28-29), James brings a sacred text into the dialogue and debate about inclusion of the Gentiles. Scripture is often a primary norm in the work of theological reflection. We ask ourselves, or the pastor asks the group, "What does the Bible say about this?" or "How do the Scriptures inform us?" The goal is not to proof-text and prop up one's position but to genuinely search and seek the direction of God's word.

Tradition is another norm that we can and should bring into dialogue when engaged in the work of theological reflection. In the case of our "everybody's welcome" situation from Acts, we might think about the tradition of God's people making provision for the alien and the foreigner in their midst (Leviticus 19:9-10). We might recall God's promise to Abraham to bless him, and through him all nations (Genesis 18:18). Tradition includes the teaching of the church or faith fathers and mothers. Your congregation may be part of a particular denominational tradition that has bearing on how you share ministry. As we recently shared a congregational dialogue about worship, one of the participants asked, "Isn't there a Baptist playbook on how to do worship?" People smiled and laughed but understood that he was asking, "What does our tradition say about worship?" It was good question. Do any of your traditions speak to the change issues you are facing? It might be worth looking at your history to see how change was interpreted in prior periods.

Finally, the third leg of the theological reflection stool is experience. Peter, Paul, and Barnabas were well-qualified to speak from their own experience when it came to God's inclusion of the Gentiles. They had witnessed persons of non-Jewish heritage come to faith in Christ, be baptized and filled with the Spirit, and live faithful lives. By the time of the Jerusalem Council, house churches filled with diverse populations had sprung up throughout Asia Minor. It was difficult to argue with these personal experiences and the weight of their witness.

As you work with your group toward change, persons will have many experiences with the topics you discuss. Some will be first-hand (primary) experiences; others, secondary, such as the report of a friend or something they've read or seen. Persons like to share their experiences, particularly if you create a climate in which such sharing is encouraged and listening is fostered. The key is being able to discern what parts of those experiences are translatable to your context and current situation.

We believe that working at change through a thoughtful pace that is conducive to theological reflection will be helpful to any community of faith. These are the tools native to our toolbox as followers of Christ. Bringing the input of Scripture, tradition, and experience into dialogue will help us begin to sort methods from message and motive from manipulation. We will need to determine which of the three norms holds more weight in our dialogue—Scripture, tradition, or experience—and how that may sway our thinking and outcome.

Perhaps an example would be helpful. We participated in a recent congregational engagement session around the topic of adult faith formation, or discipleship. The concern that was raised, which led to this discussion and some proposed change, was the notable decline in a traditional Sunday School model for younger generations in the church. While the traditional Sunday morning model continues to be vibrant, popular, and successful for the oldest generations (those in the mid-sixty to ninety age range), it has not shown the same consistent outcomes with persons age sixty and under. A congregation which once boasted seven active adult classes now has four or five, depending on the Sunday, with one group struggling to maintain teachers, and others showing inconsistent attendance throughout the year. What to do?

A recommendation for change was presented to address the deficiency in adult faith formation, particularly among the younger adults. The recommendation was to introduce small-group opportunities that might meet on times other than Sunday morning and in locations other than the church facility. This recommendation was not to discontinue the Sunday School for those for whom it worked, but to bolster efforts in discipleship with adults through other means that might be more appealing. How, then, do we apply the above norms to this discussion in order to arrive at a theologically reflective decision?

Scripture tells us that adult faith formation, or spiritual growth, is important (Acts 2:42; John 15:1-17). We are to be students of the Word of God (Psalm 1:1-2; 119:11; James 1:22). Jesus himself was a teacher who called persons in response to the gospel through his preaching and teaching. Our biblical witness clearly points to the importance of discipleship and spiritual growth and the benefit of lifelong faith formation.

Our congregation also comes from a tradition that has valued adult faith formation. Sunday School, a mid-week Bible study, occasional elective classes, retreats, and seminars have all been used and valued as part of our congregation's tradition. We are part of the many churches that adopted the Sunday School model for Christian education some 100 years ago. (It was of interest to some in our discussion that this particular tradition only dates back some 100 years!)

As our discussion evolved, persons' particular experiences (primary and secondary) with both the current Sunday School model, and the proposed additional small-group model, began to be voiced. Some expressed concern that change would impact the current practice which they found to be both helpful and important. Others expressed frustration with the current model, because they were part of a class that was less than consistent and vibrant. Some had children in other churches who had ongoing positive experiences with small-group participation. The congregation as a whole had two earlier experiences with small groups to draw upon: a mostly successful one that had happened two years prior for a six-week period, and the other, a mixed success (depending on one's perspective and experience), which had occurred several years before. In our dialogue, it was important to differentiate these two group experiences in terms of how the groups were formed and how long they lasted. One had voluntary sign-ups with clear beginning and ending boundaries; the other, which involved little personal choice, was open-ended time-wise and divided the congregation into assigned groups primarily for fellowship and care ministry.

Other factors, of course, weighed into this dialogue, including the impact on child and youth faith formation, the impact of small groups on other church ministries (such as music), and the perspective shared by busy younger adults who live with full schedules and a pace that is not conducive to regular weekend participation.

As we write, this change issue is not completely resolved or without ongoing concerns. However, for the purpose of illustrating how the above norms of Scripture, tradition, and experience have been part of the decision, we would suggest that the scriptural call to faith formation carries greater weight than even a 100-year-old tradition. This leads us to conclude that the means by which discipleship and faith formation occur should be secondary to the message that it must continue to occur. Therefore, we will continue to live our way into new practices of faith as we learn by trial and error.

A Final Word of Encouragement

Change takes time. Change involves hard work. Change is all around us. Failing to prepare the church for change will not keep change from occurring. Leaders who are active in ministry today have little choice but to become equipped to lead through change.

We have tried to demonstrate in this review of the eight great paradigm shifts found in Scripture how change always has been part of the people of God's experience. God's people have been an adaptive people whom God has walked with through change. We believe God continues to walk with us through change today.

We hope as you have read these chapters, and perhaps discussed them with a leadership team in your ministry or church, that you have been encouraged to take the discussion to a deeper level. We hope you have been encouraged by knowing you are not alone when it comes to facing change. We hope you have been encouraged to do the work of preparation as you invite others into whatever change process lies ahead. Remember this: God is at work in the midst of God's people. For that reason alone, our future is bright.

Questions for Group Discussion or Individual Reflection

1. Reflect on church traditions that have changed over the years, and use the following phrase to do so: "In the church, we used to ______, but now we______." Describe how that change happened.

2. In this chapter, we discussed the pace or rate at which adaptive change takes root. What change are you working toward that has taken place over time? How do you determine the pace at which you pursue this change?

3. Peter, Paul, and the other early church leaders had particular experiences that confirmed for them that the change (everybody's welcome) that they pursued was led of God. This included the experience of Pentecost and other ministries among the Gentiles (Acts 10). Think back over your life or the life of your congregation. Can you point to evidence of God's confirmation that has helped you make changes? What examples can you point to? At what pace did the change happen?

4. The Jerusalem Council was a pivotal event in the change described in this chapter (Acts 15). When have you been part of such an experience where parties sat down together and agreed that old ways of thinking and behaving would be replaced by new ways? What was the outcome?

5. Which of the three factors described in the chapter have the greatest impact on the pace of change in your context: 1) the size and complexity of the challenge being faced, 2) the composition of the group being led through the change, or 3) the leadership style of those involved? How does identifying that factor help you rethink your pace and your approach?

6. Where do we hear debates and dissensions that may reflect the fact that the "old" and "new" paradigms identified in this chapter are still being discussed? How are these discussions part of your congregation?

Notes

1. Gary V. Nelson and Peter M. Dickens, *Leading in Disorienting Times: Navigating Church and Organizational Change* (Duluth, GA: Chalice Press: TCP Books, 2015), 65.

2. Scot McKnight, *A Fellowship of Differents: Showing the World God's Design for Life Together* (Grand Rapids, MI: Zondervan, 2014), 14.

3. Eugene H. Peterson *A Long Obedience in the Same Direction* (Downers Grove, IL: Intervarsity Press, 1980 or 2000 2nd ed.).

4. Jim Powell, *Dirt Matters: The Foundation for a Healthy, Vibrant, and Effective Congregation* (Bloomington, IN: Westbow Press, 2013), 33.

5. In Galatians 2:1-10, Paul speaks of coming before the leaders of the Jerusalem church—including James, Cephas, and John—fourteen years after an earlier visit with Peter. The purpose of Paul's visit appears to be to share an account of his ministry to the Gentiles with the church leaders. Though the meeting results in gaining the leaders' endorsement, consider the length of time that was involved—seventeen years after Paul's conversion, and fourteen years after an early visit with Peter.

6. Dan's story about the HVAC system is one that has played out in many congregations over the last decades, and often strong opinions have companioned the change process. It is amusing to note that Dan's father-in-law was one who held such a strong opinion when the topic of adding air conditioning surfaced in his small church. Being opposed to the idea of purchasing an HVAC system for reasons of expense and thrift, he volunteered to chair the committee that would make the recommendation for or against it. Then he never called a meeting of that committee; therefore, they never had the opportunity to vote!

7. Peter Oakes, *Reading Romans in Pompeii: Paul's Letter at Ground Level* (Minneapolis: Fortress, 2009), 96.

8. William Barclay, *The Daily Study Bible Series: The Acts of the Apostles* (Philadelphia: Westminster Press, 2nd ed. 1955), 124–125.

Epilogue

In the summer of 2018, I (Dan) had the privilege of a three-month sabbatical leave. One blessing that this time away from pastoral leadership responsibilities afforded me was the opportunity to be a guest in worship with eleven different congregations. The churches that I visited, located in the United States and in the British Isles, were of different traditions, styles of worship, and ethnic diversity. Despite these differences, it was immediately obvious that each congregation was in the midst of change. Some of the churches appeared to be further along in the change process than others, but each was trying to figure out how to be the church today in their individual contexts. Conversations that I held after worship with pastors and other ministry staff and lay leaders consistently supported this observation.

Throughout this book, we have shared the ongoing change story of the First Baptist Church of Columbus, Indiana, the congregation that we call home. As I have returned from sabbatical to rejoin this body of believers, I have been able to tell them that we are not alone in working through a change process. Neither are you. Having company, however, does not necessarily make the process any easier.

We continue to learn in our context from trial and error, taking steps forward and back in our own change work. Change seldom comes as quickly as hoped or envisioned, particularly for those who are immersed in leading the change. While I applaud the congregation for their overall embrace of the need for change, and their willingness to go along with many of the experiments we've introduced in order to explore change, I confess that as a leader I grow weary from the slow pace at which we implement change. I understand that it is healthier to move at a slower pace in order to create ownership within the congregation, but often I retrace my steps, having been out in front, to re-join others and bring them along. Hence, while I wish I could report that we've reached our end goal and realized all of our hopes and dreams for change as a congregation, in reality I sense that the change process that we are in the midst of will continue to play out for quite some time.

I also find that the resistance to change, which surfaces on occasion, no matter how slight, often feels personally defeating. Part of my inner work as a leader is, therefore, to make sure I am in tune with my own emotions, keeping up with my own spiritual, mental, and physical health, and finding ways to deal with the stress that leading change creates.

A further personal observation would be that as one leads change and invites persons into a change process there is a tremendous need to stay connected. I have discovered that being the leader who both introduces and helps design the change process has clearly identified me with that process. As a consequence, I believe that persons are less inclined to tell me what they truly think, perhaps not wanting to disappoint me, or not feeling they have permission to disagree. It is important, therefore, to create additional avenues of input and feedback, and to have other leaders seek that feedback so that the pastor alone is not the sole driver of the process. Also, it is important to stay connected to congregants throughout the process so that as pastor I may continue to provide congregational leadership and care beyond the work of change.

Finally, I would simply acknowledge that it would have been far easier and much less taxing to have continued in a status-quo manner of ministry, rather than risk upsetting the congregational system (which is a necessary component to change). I have put in longer hours, attended more meetings, tossed and turned through sleepless nights, and grieved the departure of persons who have disagreed and withdrawn from the congregation or boycotted one or more of our ministry experiments. But I also have witnessed a congregation that has new energy, greater lay participation in ministry decisions and implementation, new faces, and a resurgence of hope for its future. I am confident that, by God's grace, we will continue to find our way forward into a promising and hopeful tomorrow.

Let me end with a story. One weekend during my sabbatical leave I was able to visit two congregations on the same Sunday morning. I cannot recall a time when I felt more like having experienced worship whiplash! The first congregation was made up of young people (I had to be about the oldest) who met in an urban warehouse-converted worship space and shared an energetic, fast-paced, loud, and enthusiastic time of worship. I was warmly welcomed and given a welcome gift and voucher for free coffee and pastry at their café, and I quickly grabbed a seat as the crowd gathered for worship. This church, with roots that go back to the mid-1970s, made an intentional effort toward change several years ago, and currently it is bearing fruit in a multi-campus, multiple worship service manifestation.

Just a few blocks away in that same city, I joined another congregation for worship in a beautiful, century-old, gothic cathedral-style space. I took note of the sign out front which read, "We love to meet new people," yet as I made my way down the aisle toward the front of the sanctuary (which was mandatory as the back two-thirds of the pews had been roped off) I noticed that I was among the youngest of the few persons who had gathered that morning for worship. The service was familiar and seemed authentic, yet as it came to a close, aside from one person, no one spoke to me. I even made an intentional effort to introduce myself to the pastor, but he seemed a bit annoyed by my intrusion and made some reference to visitors who come to see the architecture. The problem was I wasn't there to see the architecture.

It occurred to me that this congregation, like so many others, is probably aware of their need to change in order to better connect with their context. They may even be aware that they don't do a very good job of living up to what they put on their sign. The people who regularly gather are likely very kind and good people, and perhaps I caught them on a bad day, but were I a local resident, I would not return. The experience did, however, cause me to look with fresh eyes at the ways our congregation welcomes guests. It also re-energized my own determination to continue to work with others toward change, and it made me thankful to be among a people who understand the importance of such work.

We hope the inclusion of this epilogue—offered in honest and personal reflection from a church in the midst of change—will be an encouragement to the reader wherever it is you find yourself leading and participating in change. Remember, God's future is among God's people. Keep the faith. Our Lord is faithful.

Appendix A

Illusions of Change

If a paradigm shift is a change in how one sees, understands, or thinks about things, often part of that shift is visual. To demonstrate paradigm shifts in a visual way, consider the images that appear below. Each one can be seen in two ways. To say it another way, each image contains two objects. What do you see?

Appendix B

Terms and Types of Change

Continuous or incremental change: This is change for which we have prior experience or knowledge. We recognize a need or deficiency and apply that knowledge toward improvement. The basic evolution of drinking water in our Western society illustrates continuous change. Purifying water through filtered pitchers has evolved to the consumer buying bottles of water. How many of us twenty years ago ever thought we'd pay to buy a plastic bottle filled with water!

Tactical or technical change: This is change that is related to a particular skill or function. It does not require much in the way of creativity or process. The computer system crashed; someone with technical skill is called in to troubleshoot and fix the problem.

Discontinuous change: This is change for which we do not have prior experience or knowledge. It presents an adaptive challenge, calling for a prayerful and thoughtful process of engagement. Over time a solution may emerge, but experimentation will often be part of the process.

Change in a complicated system: This type of change, while complicated, is still fully predictable. Most often it is built on scientific discovery. For example, sending a rocket to the moon is complicated, but persons have expertise and skill today to accomplish this feat. It requires following the right formulas, building on prior knowledge and experience, and a high level of expertise in a variety of fields. Over time and with discipline, the objective can be met.

Change in a complex system: This type of change is complex and often unpredictable. It involves organic, ever-changing systems. For example, it is like rearing a child. Having done it once does not guarantee that the next time will be the same. Child-rearing formulas have some, but limited application, and prior success does not assure similar outcomes. While expertise can contribute to success, it is neither necessary nor sufficient to ensure success because every child is unique and must be understood as an individual. Relationships are important. The process is challenging but rewarding throughout.

Self-Organization: This is a grassroots, bottom-up, emergent means of organization that draws on the contributions of many versus a single or executive leader. As it applies to congregational life, self-organization is rooted in the belief that churches are living systems (the body of Christ) made up of flesh-and-blood people, gifted in unique ways, and with differing life experiences and skills. Leaders who work in the midst of the organic system encourage that system's natural growth and adaptation to fulfill God's mission. A leader's principal role in this system is to help the organism understand its identity (core values, bedrock beliefs) and mission (participation with God) while giving permission for the creativity of God's people to emerge, self-organize, and live into that mission.

Cultural change: This is change in norms, beliefs, values, and brand.

Vision change: This is change in where you are headed. It is a change in direction.

Program change: This is change in events, offerings, and ministries to support the vision.

Incarnational: This is a term used to describe the embodiment of ministry to and with others in the name of Christ. As Jesus became the Word made flesh and dwelt among us, we (in his name) embody his ways and pitch our tents in the world.

Adaptive Challenge: This is a challenge in which one has no prior experience or knowledge, therefore necessitating an adaptive approach.

Appendix C

Questions for Group Discussion or Individual Reflection

The following are additional questions that may be helpful for individuals to ponder as they read and reflect on chapters 1–8 and prepare for small-group discussion.

Chapter One: New Wineskins

1. Turn to Appendix A and spend some time looking at the illusions that appear there. Each is a picture that can be seen in two ways. Can you identify both objects in the picture? Use this as a discussion starter with your group.

2. Which of Jesus' comparisons in this story do you most identify with: A physician among the sick? A bridegroom among the wedding feast? Why?

3. How do you feel about rummage sales? Do you agree with Phyllis Tickle's assessment that we, as the church, are in the midst of a 500-year rummage sale? Where do you see evidence of this? Where is the evidence not as compelling?

4. Which of the three rummage sale results can you see emerging today? a. A new and more vital form of faith emerges; b.The organized expressions of faith are reconstituted into purer and less-ossified types of their former selves; c. Faith spreads when the overly established form of faith is broken up.

Chapter Two: Incarnation

1. Name something you do differently now than how you did it when you were much younger.

2. What is John the Baptist's role in the paradigm shift of faith discussed in this chapter? (See John 1:6-9.) Where would you place John on the Bell Curve of Change?

3. How would you summarize the Gospel writer John's intentions by what he writes in John 1:1-18? What does he want to convince his reader of? How does his account differ from the Christmas story told by Matthew and Luke (Matthew 1:18-25; Luke 2:1-20)?

4. How might we in the church apply this understanding of the incarnation to our own lives? (See 1 Corinthians 12:27; 2 Corinthians 3:1-3.) Do other Scriptures come to mind?

Chapter Three: Born Again

1. Why would Jesus be surprised that Nicodemus "...did not understand these things"? (vs. 10). What hindrances must have made it difficult for Nicodemus to understand?

2. What is your understanding of Jesus' words about being 'born again'? Is this a phrase you are comfortable using? Why or why not?

3. Verse 8 compares being "born of the Spirit" to the wind blowing. What is the point Jesus is making? What experience with wind have you had that illustrates this?

4. If you were to teach or preach this text this coming Sunday, what would be your main point(s) for your congregation? Why?

Chapter Four: Kingdom Manifesto

1. When have you heard or voiced the question: "How could this have happened?"

2. Can you think of an example of your church having moved from the center of community life toward the margins? How has your congregation responded to this move?

3. What is Jesus implying about his audience when he uses the Parable of Salt and Light in Matthew 5:13-16?

4. What are the two dominant themes in Matthew 5:17-20? Why does Jesus deal with these issues at this point?

Chapter Five: Old and New Covenants

1. There are five major covenants found in the Old Testament that are mentioned in this chapter. Can you list them and identify where they are found in Scripture?

2. In Jeremiah 31:31-34, the prophet announces a "new covenant." What are the two major promises included with this new covenant? Who fulfills this covenant?

3. Imagine the difficulty of the Jewish faithful as they heard the inherent change in understanding the "new" covenant introduced through Jesus. What difficulties or challenges face congregations today as they strive to make changes?

4. The Lord's Supper (or communion) is the ultimate confirmation of the paradigm shift from the *old* to *new* covenant discussed in this chapter. How does your faith community emphasize this act of worship as a renewal of covenant? How might you?

Chapter Six: Resurrection

1. Who are we introduced to in Luke 23:55—24:3, and what are they doing that provides the context and setting for this passage?

2. What was their state of mind? What happened to cause that state of mind? Who do they meet? What do they learn?

3. Several women are mentioned. Who were they? What did they do about what they experienced? How was it received? (See also Mark 16:11 and John 20:1-10.)

4. What day is it in Luke 24:13? Who were the travelers and where had they come from? Who joins them on their walk to Emmaus?

5. What questions does the "stranger" ask the travelers? What amazes them about him? Why do you think they could not recognize him as Jesus?

6. When their "eyes were opened," as Jesus sat with them and broke bread and blessed it, these travelers had an experience of the risen Christ. How do they describe their feelings, and what did they do next, and why?

Chapter Seven: Pentecost

1. How are the following Old Testament passages related to Pentecost: Leviticus 23:15-22, Exodus 23:16, and Numbers 28:26?
2. How long was Jesus with the disciples after the resurrection? What was their dominant concern during this time? (See Acts 1.)
3. How does the story of many languages at Pentecost reflect an Old Testament story found in Genesis 11:1-9?
4. How do you know if the change trigger is of the Spirit or just of human initiative?
5. How do you respond to the question, "Have you been filled with the Holy Spirit?"

Chapter Eight: Everybody Welcome!

1. Who were the two leaders at the center of the paradigm shift described in this chapter? What groups of people are they responsible for? What is the belief that is being challenged? (See Galatians 2:8.)
2. How was Peter prepared to accept this paradigm shift? Identify the verses in Acts 10 that show his struggle with the old paradigm and those that show his affirmation of the new.
3. How would you describe Paul's sermon in Acts 13:13-52? How did the people respond?
4. How many years have passed since the original inclusion of the Gentiles at Pentecost and the Jerusalem Council in Acts 15? What does this length of time suggest about leading change?
5. Who are the voices that participate in the Jerusalem Council (Acts 15)? Which ones affirm the new paradigm of inclusion? What is their argument based on? How is it received?
6. Read Galatians 3:23-29 and Philemon. How do these texts illustrate how the new paradigm is at the very center of early Christian teaching?

Appendix D

Church Covenant First Baptist Church, Columbus, Indiana

PREAMBLE: On the basis of our belief, the following covenant is a statement of our pledge of intent regarding faithfulness, witnessing, and relationships.

Having been led, as we believe, by the spirit of God, to receive the Lord Jesus Christ as our Savior; and, having been baptized in obedience to Christ's command as a public profession of our faith in him,

We do now, in the presence of God, Angels, and this fellowship, sincerely and joyfully enter into covenant with one another, as one body in Christ. We personally pledge, by the aid of the Holy Spirit, to walk together in Christian love; to strive for the advancement of this Church in knowledge, holiness, and caring;

To promote its growth and spirituality, to sustain its worship, ordinances, disciplines, and doctrines; to faithfully be present, and to be dedicated in our efforts to advance the Kingdom of our Savior.

To contribute cheerfully and regularly to the support of the expenses of the Church, the relief of the poor, and the spread of the Gospel through all nations.

We also pledge to maintain family and personal devotions; to educate our children in the Christian faith, to seek the salvation of our family and acquaintances;

To seek to walk correctly in the world; to be just in our dealings, faithful in our commitments, and be Christian examples in our behavior. We pledge to refrain from the promotion and use of those things which harm the body or defile the mind.

We further pledge to watch over one another in brotherly love;

to remember each other in prayer; to aid each other in sickness and distress; to cultivate Christian sympathy in feeling and courtesy in speech; to be slow to take offense, but always ready for reconciliation, and mindful of the teachings of our Savior, to secure it without delay.

Upon leaving this fellowship, we will, as soon as possible, unite with some other Church, where we can carry out the spirit of this covenant and the principles of God's Word.